Guide
Netherlands
Open-Air Museum
Arnhem

Uitgeverij Special Images b.v., Enschede 1990

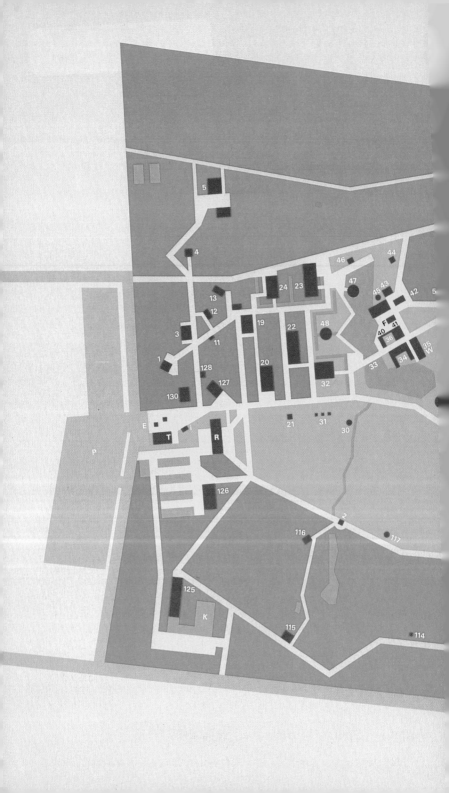

Netherlands Open-Air Museum
Plan of the Museum

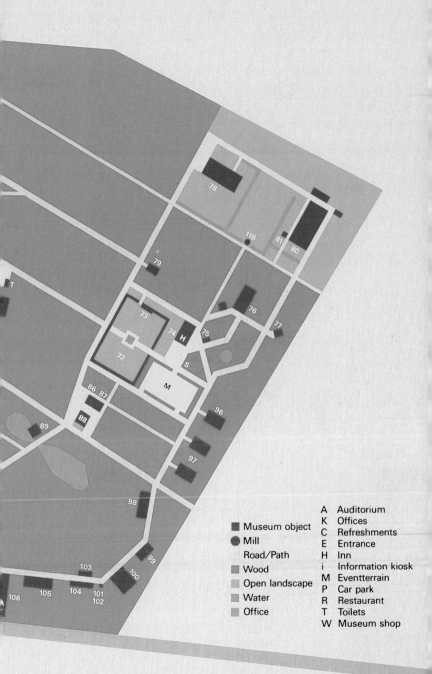

Museum object

Mill

Road/Path

Wood

Open landscape

Water

Office

A   Auditorium
K   Offices
C   Refreshments
E   Entrance
H   Inn
i   Information kiosk
M   Eventterrain
P   Car park
R   Restaurant
T   Toilets
W   Museum shop

Origin of the museum objects

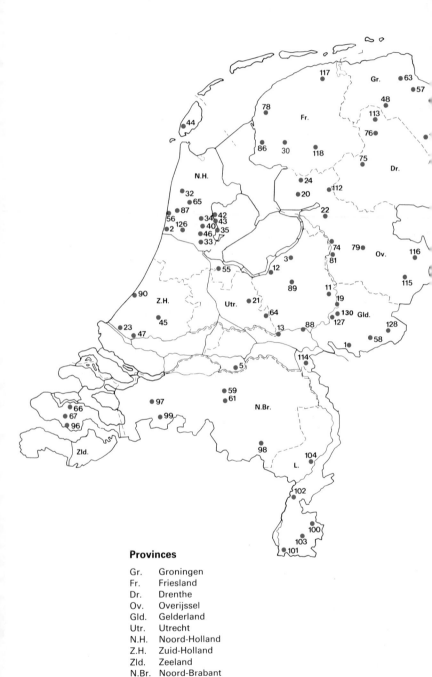

Provinces

Gr.	Groningen
Fr.	Friesland
Dr.	Drenthe
Ov.	Overijssel
Gld.	Gelderland
Utr.	Utrecht
N.H.	Noord-Holland
Z.H.	Zuid-Holland
Zld.	Zeeland
N.Br.	Noord-Brabant
L.	Limburg

Red route

Duration: 1½ - 2 hours
The red route goes along a number of important museum buildings in the middle of the park. The restaurant, inn, and museum shop also lie along the route.

Netherlands Open-Air Museum
Plan with tours

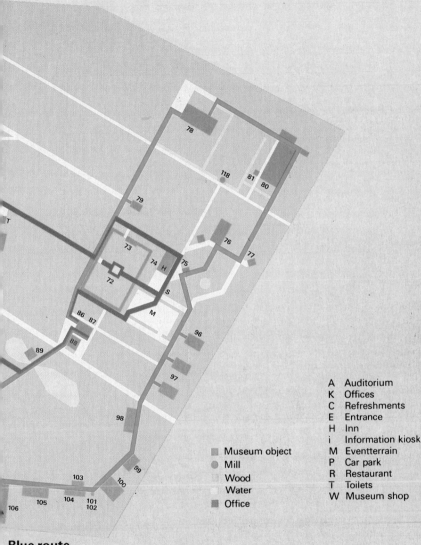

A Auditorium
K Offices
C Refreshments
E Entrance
H Inn
i Information kiosk
M Eventterrain
P Car park
R Restaurant
T Toilets
W Museum shop

■ Museum object
● Mill
Wood
Water
■ Office

Blue route

Duration: 3 - 4 hours
Undulating terrain, unpaved paths.
The blue route covers the whole museum
park (44 hectares) and goes along nearly all
the museumbuildings including the
auditorium (slide show), exhibitions,
restaurant, inn, and museum shop.

Foreword

The museum guide has been put together to form a manual, reference book, and souvenir for the visitor. In it you will find descriptions of the many attractive objects that you can discover during your stroll through our museum. There are old houses and business premises from all over The Netherlands. They have been transferred to the museum – often stone by stone – along with the furnishings, tools, and pieces of equipment that belonged with them.

The many buildings and objects, that the museum has acquired, described, and conserved since it was founded in 1912, belong to our material and cultural heritage. Together with the exhibitions scattered over the museum terrain, especially the exhibition of costumes, they tell us about the past, about the life and work of previous generations, of our parents and grandparents, and reveal the roots of the ever changing world we live in.

For your walk through the museum park there is a choice of two routes set out on the map. The buildings and other objects of interest are given in numerical order. Using these numbers it is easy to orientate yourself.

Alongside the buildings, it is worth while to pay attention to the natural surroundings, the farm yards, the new lay-out of the herb garden and its historical monastery garden, the seventeenth century cultivation where the meadows opposite the restaurant now are, the glacial ridge with spring, and the animals in the landscape.

The Netherlands Open-Air Museum contains more than we can show you on your walk through the park. Our library and documentation department offer considerable perspective for finding the answer to questions that you may have.

The museum would be pleased to be of any further assistance to you.

F.J.M. van Puijenbroek

◀ *Sculpture of 'Faam' in the garden of the Merchant's house from Koog aan de Zaan (34)*

9

The changing pattern of daily life

Founding

The Netherlands Open Air Museum was founded in 1912. A number of individuals, who were concerned about the rapid tempo in which, as a result of increasing industrialisation, a great wealth in traditions and regional diversity was under threat, took the initiative to set up an Open Air Museum in The Netherlands. They took as their example establishments in Sweden, Norway and Denmark, especially Skansen near Stockholm (1891) and the Friland Museum near Copenhagen (1901).

Following the leasing of a large 30 hectare terrain from Arnhem Council in 1914, later extended to 44 hectares, and having transferred six buildings there, the Open Air Museum opened its gates to the public for the first time on July 13, 1918. Since then characteristic buildings from all parts of The Netherlands have found their way to the museum.

War years

After its first thirty years the museum had justified its existence, and in 1941 the state itself took on the responsibility. The Netherlands Open-Air Museum became then the National Folk Museum. The original society 'The Netherlands Open-Air Museum' now found its dynamic continuation in the Society of Friends of The Netherlands Open-Air Museum.

During the war years the museum had a precarious existence. The Battle of Arnhem in 1944 with the upheaval of the town cannot be ignored. For a hundred days the museum offered refuge to evacuees, until acts of war drove them away. The hostilities caused a lot of destruction in the museum. Several buildings and parts of the collection were lost, including the whole historical costume collection.

Recovery

Everything possible was done to repair the damage to the museum buildings and park. After the re-opening in 1946 the museum attracted 57.000 visitors. From the outset the collection of costumes has consisted of two parts: one part which is the property of the museum, and the other a collection, which was given for the museum to manage by the Royal Family. On the occasion of the Golden Jubilee of Queen Wilhelmina in 1948, a national committee had collected afresh a representative collection of regional costumes. At the same time the museum brought its own collection once more up to an appropriate standard for a museum. The result of all these efforts culminated in 1955 with the opening of a new exhibition building. The first exhibition bore the title 'The Netherlands in Wedding Attire'. In that year the museum had more than 250.000 visitors.

Expansion

In the years after the war the collection quickly expanded with farms, windmills, and industries from all parts of the country being added. On April 24, 1962 the Open-Air Museum celebrated its Golden Jubilee. The 'Friends' presented the so called 'Bee house', in which the tools of traditional beekeeping are permanently on show. In this Jubilee year more than 440.000 visitor came.

On January 9, 1971, a fierce fire, the cause of which remained a mystery, destroyed a part of the Zaan area, as a result of which the cobbler's house, the tobacco shop, and the corner house from Krommenie were lost. The first two buildings proved impossible to replace.

Double drawbridge from Ouderkerk aan de Amstel (33)

Instead a small garden was laid out and a coach house with a coach man's house were constructed. One building, obtained in Zaandam after the fire, acquired the function of souvenir shop. At several places in the museum exhibition areas have been created, such as in the hall situated next to the auditorium, near the herb garden, and in the 'Vlaamse schuur' of the farmhouse from Brabant. Objects and tools from the museum's extensive depots, supported by drawings and prints from our own documentation department and print collection, provide illumination on particular facts of daily life.

11

Objective

The objective of The Netherlands Open-Air Museum is to give a historically accurate picture of the changing pattern of daily life in The Netherlands from about 1600. To this end original houses, farms, windmills, and business premises have been rebuilt in the museum park. As far as possible they are located and fitted up in suitable surroundings and with the appropriate furniture, utensils, and tools. Since it was founded eighty buildings have been transferred and rebuilt on the museum terrain.

Originally the accent in the Open-Air Museum lay on living and working in the traditional society until around 1880: the farmer, the shepherd, the fisherman, and the craftsman stood central. Today in the Open-Air Museum we interpret the concept of folk history much more widely. Attention is given to townsfolk, labourers and their accomodation, and to monuments of industry and technology, also known as 'industrial archeology'. In this way in 1978 the museum acquired the steam sawmill Nahuis in Groenlo, which has been preserved in situ. At the museum itself the commercial depot of the firm of Massee from Goes sprang up, and the steam dairy factory Freia from Veenwouden is among the future plans. In this way the collection activities of the museum have been extended to include the twentieth century. The farmstead from Groningen for example has a 1930's interior.

The picture of daily life, which the Open-Air Museum tries to give, is not only evoked by the position and lay-out of buildings in the museum park.

Artist's impression of a presentation about butter and cheese making in a steam powered dairy

Additional information in exhibitions, publications, audio-visual programmes, and guided tours are also important means of bringing the knowledge across and of establishing an image for the public.

Friesian curved panelled gig, c. 1875

1 Horse-driven oil mill, Zieuwent (Gld.)

Installation for pressing out oil from seeds. From around 1830 an old farmhouse accomodated this mechanised small business.

The trade it did was nothing like that built up by establishments like the bleachery at Overveen (56) or the sawmills of North and South Holland (47), but it was fairly important locally since the oil it produced was needed for lighting as well as baking and frying. The oil was pressed from various types of oilseed, such as rapeseed and flaxseed, which were cultivated by most farmers, usually smallholders, in areas like the Achterhoek (eastern) region of Gelderland. The seed was brought to the mill by the farmer, who paid the miller a fee and in return got not only his rape oil and linseed oil (from flax) but also residual products like rape cake and linseed cake which he could use for cattle feed. The miller, like most other village craftsmen in the east and south of the country, ran a smallholding of his own too.

The power to drive mills like this was provided by a horse (or sometimes an ox) which because it had to keep going round in circles had to be blinkered, and because of the enormous strain involved had to be changed every two hours. The horse was harnessed to a pole connected to the shaft of the crusher, which consisted of two heavy stone wheels designed to crush the seeds to a pulp. From here the pulp was transferred to a stove, where it was heated with constant stirring in order to increase the yield of oil during the actual press-

Nose bag

ing. The stirring mechanism was driven from the heavy horizontal shaft mounted above the beams, which in turn was geared to the shaft of the crusher. The heated pulp was then poured into woollen bags with leather facings and the bags were placed in the huge wooden press, where they were repeatedly stamped by a wedge hammered home by a machine rather like a double pile-drive. Essentially this comprised of two heavy upright balks (the stamps), each of which was raised in turn by the gearing at the end of the horizontal shaft and then allowed to fall again under its own weight. One of the stamps hammered the wedge responsible for the pressing, while the other struck an inverted wedge in order to knock the first one free again. All in all, it was a noisy business which could be heard all over the neighbourhood. The oil thus produced was collected in pans placed under the press, the average output for a ten to twelvehour day being about forty litres.

In many areas oil presses were also installed in wind-mills and water-mills, in which the machinery may have been a little more complicated but the principle was the

Leather-faced press bag

same. In country districts these mills were generally local businesses with a strong tradition of craftsman-ship, and some may even have been run in conjunction with a corn mill. In the more industrialized coastal area in the west of the country, however, where there were numerous oil mills scattered amongst all the other in-dustrial mills, they were much larger and more sophisti-cated and the craft tradition was entirely lacking. There is one still in operation and open to visitors, in the *Zaanse Schans*, near Zaandijk.

Literature: A.J. Bernet Kempers, Oliemolens, 1979. With

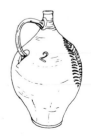

Pitcher

a summary in English (available in museum shop and kiosk).

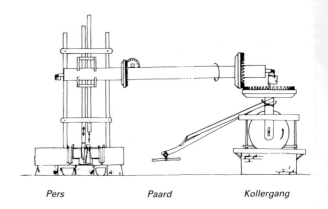

Pers   Paard   Kollergang

2 Fowler's hut, Aerdenhout (N.H.)

Equipment for catching birds is set up in this hut.

Since the fifteenth century prosperous inhabitants of Holland used a 'vinkenbaan' to catch small birds for consumption. In the following centuries this means of catching birds developed into a national sport. The well-to-do amused themselves with it, while the ordinary man had a welcome addition to his income. Mainly songbirds, such as chaffinches, bramblings, siskins, and goldfinches were caught. The autumn migration provided for large bags. Because the migration takes place in a west-south-west to south-west direction, the fowlers' huts were built facing a north-north-east direction, with an open view over the fields. In front of the hut a path was set out with a screen along the edge. Call birds fastened on to small planks and scattered alder-cones induced down the birds flying over. A net was mostly used for capture. This net consisted of two sections, that were set next to the path. At the right moment, when the birds had settled down to feed on the cones, the fowler gave a sharp pull on his tow-line so that the sections of the net rose up and snapped shut. Inside the hut there were boards on which the total number of birds caught in a year was noted down, as well as what the largest bag in a day was and in which turn the most birds were caught.

The Bird protection Act of 1912 offered protection to birds and outlawed bird catching. In The Netherland birds are now only allowed to be caught for ringing fo the benefit of the study of their migration behaviour.

Fowler's hut, Bloemendaal (N.H.)

3   Small farmhouse, Vierhouten (Gld.)

Small farm on poor sandy soil, built shortly before 1850.
It is really more of a labourer's cottage than a farm. The
building has an aisled structure (76). The walls of the
house are brick, and the barn has brick at the back and
weatherboarding at the side.
The entrance to the barn, which has a sunken stall (76),
is at the back. Nearby are two hay barracks of different
types from Gelderland. These consist of one or more
posts with a roof, the height of which can be adjusted
according to the amount of hay stored under it.

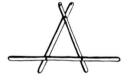

Sheep's collar

Farmhouses like this, which are really miniature
versions of the ones being built on the sandy soils at this
period, are very common on the Veluwe. This is because
in the nintheenth century there was still a lot of waste
ground here, on which numerous farm labourers were
able to settle and eventually, by dint of unremitting hard
work, to raise themselves to the level of small independent farmers.
The way in which such a farm developed is graphically
described in a government publication of 1908: 'A labourer who had just got married and had next to nothing
to his name would generally begin with a few chickens
and a goat or two, the latter being kept both for their milk
and for the dung, which he would spread on his little
field. Gradually he would take on other animals, first a
few piglets and then a calf for fattening, until eventually

Well

19

Can for extinguishing embers

he would reach the stage where he was able to keep the calf and sell the milk. The waste from the dairy, together with undersized potatoes and meal from the rye he grew, would then allow him to increase his stock of pigs, which again would bring in more money, while the extra dung would enable him to bring a bit more of the heathland under cultivation. If all went well he would gradually cut down on the amount of time he went out working for other people and devote more attention to his own farm, especially if he had grown-up children who were already earning. It did not always work out so favourably, but nonetheless the small-scale farms of labourers in this area often have a salutary effect'.

Bible text

Dog, English pottery

4 Beekeeping exhibition

Beekeeping (apiculture) used to always be an important sideline for the country population of The Netherlands. Bees were kept for their honey, which was an important sweetener before sugar came into daily use in households. Bees in the wild nest in tree hollows and the like. The oldest beehives are then also hollow tree trunks. Later hives were woven from straw and purple moorgrass. Bundles of straw were made using a ring-shaped object, for example a piece of cow's horn. These bundles were fashioned into a hive on a kind of mould and bound together with split blackberry shoots.

With the gathering of the honey the whole bee population normally used to be destroyed, the so called **slaughter** of a bee population. To prevent this the beekeeper developed the frame. This is a wooden framework, in which the bees are forced to form honeycombs. The frame is removeable, so that when gathering the honey the bee population need not be destroyed. The beekeeper can also see whenever there are new queens born. With this it is possible to ensure that a part of the population does not disappear with the old queen to form a new nest, while the new queen remains in the old hive: the so called **swarming**. This improvement had an enormous impact on the design of the hive. Eventually in this way the modern hive came into being. This hive is rectangular and has a detachable cover. A pliable material such as straw was now no longer necessary. The hive is made of wood and nowadays from synthetic material as well. Hives even exist made of polystyrene foam!

The tools used in beekeeping underwent the same changes as the hive. Old tools bear witness to tremendous adjustments and highlight local contrasts. These days however the tools are mass produced and are the same throughout nearly the whole country.

Another important product of beekeeping is the wax. This is a secretion of the bee, used to make its honeycombs. In the past wax had an important function as a light source, candles being made from it.

Haulage horse collar with 'scarf', c. 1930

St Ambrose hive, Gemert (N.B.) c. 1944, made especially for the museum

Rattle

Chair from Oirschot

Parlour | Farm kitchen | Horses | Threshing-floor | Drained stalls

5 Farmhouse, Varik (Gld.)

In this building, which was put up in 1646, the aisled (76) barn has always been divided off from the farmhouse proper. The latter has been altered at various times: the parlour was built on around 1700 and fitted with cupboard beds some time later, while the back kitchen was enlarged to its present form around 1900. These and other modifications were, for the most part, retained when the building was moved to the museum and in its present state it gives an idea of a typical farm in the Betuwe area (between the Lower Rhine and the Waal) at the end of the nineteenth century.

In this area it was traditional for the loft above the tie-beams in the barn to be reserved for hay, which was fed in through a hatch from carts standing under cover of the specially designed overhanging roof. The grain harvest was stored in a separate barn with an adjustable roof, rather like a hay barrack (3), and with storage space at ground level for farm equipment and carts. This particular example also has a lean-to round three of its sides in which pigs and calves were stalled. The stalls in the main barn were for horses (horse-breeding was traditionally an important activity in the Betuwe) and for the dairy herd.

In these stalls the animals stood on a hard and sometimes slightly raised floor (instead of in a pit, as in the sunken stall, 76) and most of their **dung** found its way into a **gutter** which was cleaned out every day. If they stood facing the threshing-floor (76), as in this barn, then the gutter ran behind the wall of the stalls and the dung was swept out through holes or flaps in the side and back walls of the barn, but if they stood facing the outside wall, then the dung was generally carried outside in wheelbarrows. Obviously this type of stall is more hygienic than the sunken type and for this reason it was adopted at an early date in major dairy-farming areas such as Friesland and North Holland. But in areas where people mainly kept cows to obtain manure, the sunken stall generally survived until the advent of artificial fertilizers in the nineteenth century.

The rich clay soils of the Betuwe were highly productive and lent themselves readily to mixed farming. Both dairy farming and meat production were long-established activities of considerable importance. Butter was made on the farms themselves (78) and on a farm of this size the milk yield was so high that a form of mechanization had to be introduced. In one of the stalls there is a large churn which was operated by a treadwheel turned by a strong dog. There was also a lot of fruit-growing and on the arable side large crops of cereal, pulses, etc. were raised, not to be used as animal feeding stuffs but to be sent to market. This diversity made for security, but on the other hand the farmers often had to contend with floods.

Large farms on the fertile river clays in the centre and east of the country thus enjoyed a continuous prosperity which made it possible to introduce into their buildings refinements unknown in poorer areas. As early as the seventeenth century, for example, the barn and the house part were not just separated by a wall but treated as separate structural entities, with the result that the farmhouse came to be more like a town house both in construction (load-bearing walls with beams set into them) and in outward appearance. This particular farmhouse originally had brick arches above the windows (they are still visible in places) and its wall clamps proclaim its date, while the citified façade even runs to a step gable over the parlour. The T-shaped plan, which results from building the farmhouse with its axis perpendicular to that of the barn, was particularly common in the Betuwe area and along the river IJssel in Gelderland in the eighteenth and nineteenth centuries. 'De Hanekamp', a farmhouse-cum-inn from Zwolle (74), which dates from c. 1750, is another example.

Reserve numbers 6-10

Cupboard

Dog churn

Headstall

Fly trap

11 Cobble-stone floor, Geesteren (Gld.)

This floor, with a separate shelter, comes from the kitchen-cum-living room of the farm 'De Stroomboer', which was devastated in the war. The edge consists of bricks, the sections are of pebbles. The year 1838 is written in it, along with two plough wheels and a few other figures, and the initials of eleven people: the farmer (LamBertus TigchelMan), his wife (eLisaBeth Roossink), children and employees. Each section contains about two hundred and fifty stones. Only the design with numbers, letters, and figures has been transferred to the museum; the entire floor had a hundred and thirty sections.

In the sixteenth century hard floor coverings with or without decorated tiles were still the preserve of house interiors belonging to the rich. In farms the floor was, even in the living quarters, mostly of loam. From the end of the seventeenth century, but especially in the eighteenth and nineteenth centuries, paving was also added there in the appropriate places, such as the kitchen-cum-living room and the paths in front of and behind the farm. This took place often using relatively cheap or readily available materials, such as brick, 'Bentheimer' sandstone (to the east of Twente), pebbles, and small strips of clay ('potscheur'), a by-product from potteries. The pebbles came from moraine deposits that were left behind in The Netherlands in the ice age by glaciers or that were transported by rivers.
Examples of cobble-stone floors are to be found among others in the museum farms from Harreveld (127), Beuningen (115), and Zeijen (76), the school from Lhee (75), and the flour mill from Delft (90).

12 Day labourer's cottage, Nunspeet (Gld.)

This one-roomed cottage, backed by a barn with a little sunken stall (76) for a goat and a sheep or two, is an improved version of the type of dwelling lived in by casual labourers. Compared with the hovels they usually lived in, the improvements here include walls of brick and wood instead of turves, and a floor of flagstones instead of mud. Refinements like these were gradually introduced towards the end of the nineteenth century and give a false impression of the standard of living of most casual labourers in the past, especially when carefully reconstructed, as in this case.
The cottage used to be lived in by casual agricultural and forestry workers from the Veluwe.

Milk can

It was originally one of a 'colony' of hovels on the heathland just outside Nunspeet. The people who lived there belonged to the weakest group of workers on the land. Each spring the whole family, like many others on the Veluwe, would go off to Friesland and Drenthe, taking the goat, the sheep and the dog with them, to strip the oak trees of their bark, vast quantities of which used to be required for tanning leather. After two and a half months of hard labour, from three in the morning to nine at night, they would go home with a bit of money in

Cooking-pot

27

Provisions box

their pockets to meet the baker's and grocer's bills. On this, plus casual work for farmers, a bit of poaching, and whatever other irregular work they could get (such as helping with the hay harvest), they had to get through the year as best they could. Casual labourers formed quite a sizeable proportion of the agricultural population and were regarded as the pariahs of rural society. Outside the seasonal peaks in the demand for labour, which they naturally made the most of, they had to fend for themselves. Rather than live in sheep-pens or pig-sties they often settled outside the villages and hamlets, like numerous other vagrants on the fringes of society, in hutments put up on the heath or sand drifts or in the woods. The existence of such hovels, and of whole colonies of huts in the eastern part of the country, is referred to by various writers in the early nineteenth century, and was tolerated because the farming system would have broken down without casual labour. Places where they were found included, for instance, Olde-broek (167 huts), Doornspijk (32), Heerde (97), Hoender-loo, near Zwolle, between Wijhe and Olst, the Achter-hoek and Hattem. The Hattem settlement is described in a publication of 1853, from which we learn that the hovels were generally in a wretched condition, with floors below ground level, walls of turves and roofs of heather. Inside there were usually a fireplace consisting of three upright stones, and a couple of wickerwork cots, in which people slept on a sack of straw or moss laid over bundles of firewood.

Day labourers' cottages in other areas were on the whole somewhat better, but they had to pay rent for them out of their extremely meagre and irregular earnings, and, as there was no waste ground, there was no game, no free firewood, and no domestic animals could be kept either. Consequently the overall situation of these labourers was often even worse than that of those on the higher ground and there was certainly no question of their being able to build up little smallhol-dings of their own(3). Some nineteenth century writers compared their plight to that of, for example, the Irish, and this was by no means exaggerated, as is clear from a report drawn up in 1880 on a visit made to the Nether-lands at the behest of the British government by a certain Jenkins, in which it is categorically stated that the wages, housing and food of the Dutch farm labourer were all much worse than those of his English counter-part.

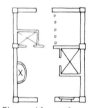

Plan and front of cottage c. 1825

13 Sheepcote, Ederveen (Gld.)

Night shelter for sheep. Outbuildings such as this used to be common on the high sandy soil extending from the eastern part of the province of Utrecht to Twente. They were sometimes situated near farmhouses, sometimes in the fields or on the heath. They would be used to house the sheep at night so that the all-important dung could be collected. In essence they were nothing more than sunken stalls (46), with roofs constructed of simple trusses (103) supported on posts driven into the ground, and with walls of wooden planks nailed to the inside of the posts. The whole thing was strengthened with turves and sometimes, as here, with adjustable braces as well. The fact that the wood eventually rotted away did not matter very much as it was easy enough to find new material. Consequently rough wooden constructions like this generally became a veritable patchwork in the course of time, as can be seen from the stalls in the little farmhouse from Vierhouten (3).

Reserve numbers 14-18

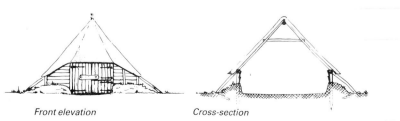

Front elevation   *Cross-section*

19　Small farmhouse, Beltrum (Gld.)

Weaver's shuttle

Farm used for a little argriculture and cottage industry. Parts of this aisled, timber-framed building (76) may date back to about 1750. All the outside walls originally had wattle-and-daub panels (103) but in the front wall these were later replaced by bricks, while the other three walls were almost completely rebuilt in brick, with mud as mortar. The gables are clad with oak planks. The original plan was probably that of a small 'los hoes' (76). It was altered to its present form in the first half of the nineteenth century.

Clothes-chest

Although it is roughly the same shape and size as the farm from Harreveld (127), this farmhous is not a 'los hoes', as there is a partition wall between the living area and the barn. Against this wall, on the kitchen side, moreover, there is a fireplace, complete with flue and chimney to take the smoke away. Life was therefore rather more comfortable here than in a 'los hoes'. Even so, it was still a very humble farm. This is obvious from a description of the area written in 1826, from which we learn that even the mud was only used as mortar in 'huts and other meagre dwellings'. Nor was the standard of living all that high, as can be judged from the fact that in 1838, for instance, this cottage housed two families, comprising no less than twelve people in all!

The kitchen has a floor made of little bricks. These were known as 'potscheur' because they were originally a by-product of the potteries in the neighbourhood. Floors of this type, as well as floors made of pebbles laid in patterns (11), used to be common in this area and just over the border.

As with the farm from Harreveld (127), it was not possible to live from agriculture alone, and in the area around Beltrum (i.e. between Zutphen and Winterswijk) textiles were one of the most important cottage industries. As early as 1700 there were merchants in places like Win-

Folding table

Gable finial

terswijk, Neede and Eibergen who, besides dealing in flax, were also beginning to engage in the actual process of manufacturing linen goods. They got poverty-stricken farmers in the hamlets to prepare the thread and do the weaving and then bleached the linen themselves before dispatching it to the west of the country and elsewhere. The textiles produced by the cottage weavers were on the coarse side, but much finer cloth was made in the larger villages, by specialist weavers who did not engage in farming activities. The looms they used were sometimes too big to go into their houses and had to be accommodated in a special building, a 'manufactory', belonging to the manufacturer. The extent of the industry can be gauged from the fact that before 1808 in Neede alone the making of linen-damasks for table use was providing work for no less than 250 people, not counting children.

Near the farmhouse is a little bread-oven (116). Bread

Chair

31

continued to be made in many households, both in town and country, until well into the nineteenth century.
In the barn are several farm carts from the eastern part of the country.

Small baker's oven from 't Woold (Gld.)

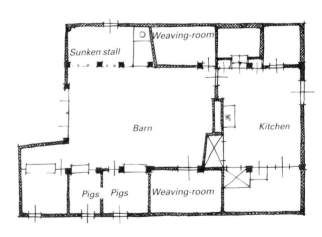

20 Farmhouse, Kadoelen (Ov.)

In the course of the eighteenth century the traditional arrangement of the aisled type of farm building, in which the barn doors were in the end wall (76), was gradually replaced by other forms, with specifically local variations. This example, which was probably erected

33

Foot-warmer

around 1800 but incorporates later alterations, is typical of the form that evolved in the district of Vollenhove, where the land was mainly pasture, with some arable. As in the Staphorst example (22), there is a hay-mow at the back of the barn and the doors to this area, as well as the even larger ones to the rest of the barn, are all built into the low side wall. The barn is separated from the living quarters by a brick wall.

Knive-grinder

In the mow the hay was stacked from floor to roof. Consequently there is no loft here and the bay between the posts (103) could be made much wider than on the threshing-floor, over which there was a loft for storing cereals. In one of the aisles are drained stalls with manure doors (5), and at the back pigsties.

There are some similarities to the Staphorst farm in the living quarters, too. In both cases, for example, the hood over the fireplace is against the front wall between the windows. The chimney here, however, is entirely of brick, and there is also a proper vestibule.

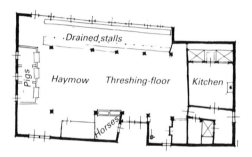

Kampereiland regional costumes, c. 1850. Water colour by V. Bing and J. Braet von Ueberfeldt

21 Dovecote, Hamersveld (Utr.)

In The Netherlands, dovecotes are found principally near old country houses. The right to keep doves was originally held exclusively by the aristocracy. The doves in the cote were not given additional food, and they sought their food from the surrounding fields, much to the displeasure of the farmers. The number of birds in a cote could vary from around ten to several thousand, so that the damage to the crops sometimes was considerable.

After the sixteenth century farmers and commoners were allowed to keep doves as well, depending upon the size of the land they occupied. Apart from for show, the doves were also kept for consumption. Their excrement found a welcome use in the growing of specialised plants such as melons, pumpkins, tobacco and hemp. This is why doves were often kept in large numbers.

Dovecotes are found throughout the whole of Europe and in large parts of Asia. Already in the Egypt of the Pharaohs the keeping of doves was known. In The Netherlands we see mainly upraised round, square or polygonal wooden cotes. The dovecote in the museum is an example of this. This cote is a replica of a cote near the farm 'Het Prinsenhof' from Hamersveld in Utrecht. It was presented to the museum by evacuees from Arnhem who in 1944 sought refuge on the museum terrain (91).

In addition to this we have in The Netherlands the dove tower, an accomodation for doves made of stone with a stone foundation. These towers can also have a variety of forms. The way they were built was not always

Small drainage mill, called an 'aanbrengertje', from Langweer (30)

straight forward, but just like the cotes the towers are graceful and constitute a decorative element in the landscape.

In The Netherlands there are about twenty-five dovecotes and just as many towers still in existence. Cotes attached to a house or lodge are a little more common. Unfortunately the free standing towers and cotes are no longer used or maintained, so that a number of these are likely to disappear in the near future.

22   Farmhouse, Staphorst (Ov.)

This very long, aisled farmhouse, mainly for the purpose of cattle farming, has brick walls in the living quarters and mostly wooden ones elsewhere. It was built around 1800.

The adjoining villages of Staphorst and Rouveen, strung along the old main road from Zwolle to Meppel, are situated at the point where the pastures on the low-lying peat soils meet the sandy soils on the higher ground. Most of the farms concentrate on raising cattle and for this they need an enormous amount of hay for winter feeding. Consequently, at the back of the barn, there is a capacious **hay-mow** where hay was stacked from floor to roof, and an entrance has been provided for the hay-carts in the low side wall. The poor, sandy soil also meant, however, that a great deal of manure was needed; so there is a large sunken stall (76) in the centre of the barn, with manure doors again in the side walls. The threshing-floor (76) between the stall and the living quarters also served as a feedway and a small corner of it was used as a scullery.

Chest from Staphorst

Though by no means conservative in other respects, the people of Staphorst have clung to old styles in their dress and houses longer than most other country folk and certainly much longer than townspeople. Even to-day their houses still retain many of the features one might have found in the past in any average farmhouse in the east of the country. For instance, the usual type of fireplace in the kitchen was, until quite recently, a direct descendant of that found in a 'los hoes' (76), with iron hearth plate and ash pit under a wooden hood and chimney. Other traditional items are the chest, the food cupboard, which was set beside the front door so as to form a sort of vestibule, the ladder-backed, rush-bottomed

Truck

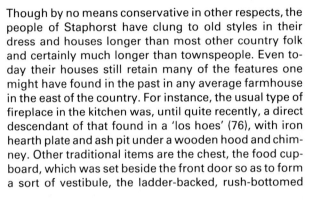

chairs, the folding table, which was propped up against the food cupboard when not in use, and the cupboard beds. Interiors like this have come to be regarded as typical of Staphorst but in fact the style only crystallized gradually from about 1850 on. Particularly characteristic

39

Painted ornament

are the tiles, which began to be used much more extensively on the floor and the walls at a time when they were already becoming less common in the rest of the country, and the painted woodwork and furniture, which were often further embellished with gay flowers, garlands and improving proverbs in a countrified version of the Biedermeier style that was fashionable in the early nineteenth century. This fashion was given considerable impetus by a German family of painters by the name of Goldsteen, who settled in nearby Meppel around 1825, but it also was partly due to the fact that the villagers were great traders, often journeying far from home, and were in the habit of picking up good solid secondhand cupboards and cabinets, to say nothing of richly ornamented eighteenth-century street doors and so forth, which were no longer fashionable in town.

They never seem to have been particularly prosperous, however. Their style of life was frugal and they did not always manage to escape poverty. Around 1850, for instance, it became difficult to collect any taxes from them since their incomes were so low. Most of them were only smallholders and they were generally obliged to seek other work besides farming. They traded in cattle, horses and indeed anything they could lay their hand on; they went off as far afield as France to work as woodcutters, or Germany to do seasonal work on the land such as haymaking; they made clogs, cut peat, worked as thatchers, carriers and so on, and the deliberations of the local council were often accompanied by the clicking of knitting-needles, since people could earn money by knitting stockings and mittens. Under these conditions it was not uncommon for the whole of the farm work to fall to the lot of the woman of the household, which meant that it was left to the grandparents to bring up the children.

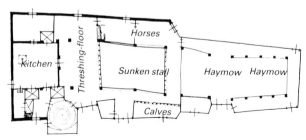

Horse mill

23 Large farmhouse, Oud-Beijerland (Z.H.)

This farmhouse, which looks more like a castle, was put up by a country landowner in 1617. He had it built with one more story than usual to accommodate a series of rooms ('the lord's rooms') which he himself retained the right to use when he wanted to go hunting or stay in the country for a while. The rest of the house was lived in by his tenant who worked the farm belonging to it on the fertile marine clays of the then newly reclaimed Hoekse Waard polders. It is built entirely of brick and in construction and style it follows contemporary town houses. The barn that originally stood behind it had long since disappeared by the time it was transferred to the museum, so a new one more or less in the style of those on the islands of South Holland has been added to give it the aspect of a farmhouse once more.

Land reclamation was a costly business, but the reclaimed soils in the area to the north of the Maas estuary (i.e. IJsselmonde, Hoekse Waard, Voorne and Putten, all of which were originally islands) were so fertile and produced such good surpluses that it was highly remunerative. The polder on which this farmhouse stood belonged to the famous Count Egmont, who lived in Brussels and figured so prominently in his country's

Farmhouse façade

Farmhouse before 1583

Wall clamps

41

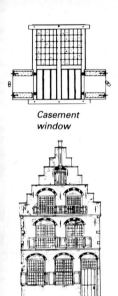

Casement window

Town house façade c. 1625

history. He had it diked in 1557. The money for empoldering was usually raised by selling off part of the new land to other very wealthy financiers (who were generally also absentee landlords) and by letting the rest to tenant farmers. The soil lent itself to mixed farming on a large scale. Here livestock and arable crops could exist independently, side by side, instead of having to support one another in a cycle of fodder and manure production as they did on the sandy soils in the east of the country. Also, the variety of crops that could be produced made people less vulnerable to changes in demand. Among the important products traditionally sent to market (often an international one) were cereals, flax (for linen weaving) and madder (for paint making). One result of all this was that the type of aisled building with a large haymow in the barn and large doors in the side walls (22) was already found in this area by about 1600. Some idea of a typical Beijerland farm of that period is given by the drawing in the margin, which is taken from a land surveyor's map of 1583.

24 Farmhouse, Giethoorn (Ov.)

This farmhouse was built in Giethoorn in 1832 and is typical of the marshy pasture and fens of north-west Overijssel.

The walls of the living quarters are mainly brick, those of the barn wood, including a wooden wall between barn and house. Most of the nave of the barn, which has an extra high roof, was used as a mow (22) for storing the enormous amount of hay required for winter feeding. The beams here are noticeably lighter than in barns where they had to support a loft. Between the haymow and the wall of the house was a general-purpose area used, among other things, for making butter and as a scullery.

Peat-cutting spade

In one of the aisles of the barn is a row of simple drained stalls (5) with a separate feedway (there being no arable farming and so no need for a sunken stall in which to collect manure). The other aisle served as a store for such things as peat for the fire. Peat was cut locally by the farmer himself and, apart from supplying his own needs, formed an important secondary source of income, along with fishing, reed-cutting, etc. The barn doors, which are in the side walls to allow for the haymow, are comparatively small. This was because wagons and carts were almost never used in Giethoorn, where the hay was brought in from the meadows in boats and carried into the barns on handbarrows. Under the overhanging eaves at one side of the barn is a row of

Churn with plunging dasher

Eelspear

beehives and, as in many other old farmhouses (e.g. at Staphorst), a sand box. Fine white sand was used for scouring pots and pans, tiles floors and steps, and every morning the flagstones inside the house were strewn with sand, sometimes, especially at weekends, in patterns.

Reserve numbers 25-29

Peat-scuttle

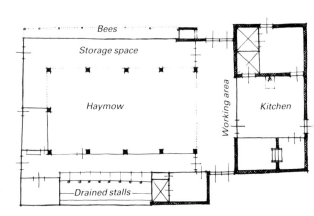

44

Het vogelschieten op Walcheren

31 Poles for shooting birds

These poles were set up in the museum for the holding of shooting competitions. In the past such events were held regularly in the museum. Nowadays such competitions still take place in North Brabant, Limburg and elsewhere. This happens mostly in spring, on the feast day of the patron saint of the club organising the event.

The participants in the competition take turns at shooting at a wooden bird or (popin) jay, which is placed on a high stake. The stake is fastened in such a way, that it just like a flag pole can be swung down to change the bird.

One shoots with a crossbow or longbow, and sometimes with a gun or rifle. Shooting down the bird or part of it earns points. The winner is allowed to call himself king.

Curd knife

Wooden bucket

32 Farmhouse, Zuid-Scharwoude (N.H.)

This building dates from 1745. It is virtually square in plan, with a square haymow (22) in the centre, and has a more or less pyramidal roof. The roof is supported by a framework of timbers resting on four massive wooden posts (103), one at each corner of the haymow. Along one side there is a row of drained stalls (5) for 18 to 20 cows, whose milk was used to make full-cream cheese. The stalls are decorated in the way they often used to be in North Holland in the summer when the cows were put out to pasture. Besides dairy farming there will have been some arable and also some market gardening. The wood paneling and tiled fireplaces in the living quarters are in a style often found in North Holland in the eighteenth century, not only in farmhouses but also in the houses of well-to-do people such as merchants and manufacturers in the Zaan area, Waterland and elsewhere.

This is another example of a structure adapted to accommodate the huge haymow that was needed to store hay for winter feeding. In this respect it may be compared with the barn at the back of the farm from Giethoorn (24). There, however, the solution was to modify the traditional structure of the building, whereas here a completely new solution has been found. The result, as is obvious from the ground plan, is a thoroughly functional design, specifically suited to the needs of this type of farm, and as such it represents one of the last phases

46

in an age-old development involving the positioning of cattle and hay. Thus the distance between the two has been minimized (especially as there are feeding hatches above the stalls) and, what is more, the heat given off by the haymow in winter has been used to good advantage by arranging the cupboard beds in brick niches round the sides. This was not the only solution, however. Other variants were developed in Friesland (78), Wieringen and the Frisian Islands, and in this connection it is inter-

Cheese-mould

esting to note that the sheepcote from Texel (44) is really nothing more than a pyramidal structure cut through the middle, with stalls arranged around a central haymow.

To make the cheese unskimmed milk was warmed over the fire and rennet was added to make it curdle. When the curds had formed, a curd knife was drawn through them to break them up so that the whey would come to the top and could be ladled off. The curds were then put

DEN 13 MAY 1745.
HEEFT *Jan Van Druyper*
OUT 2½ IAAR AAN DIT
HUYS DEN EERSTEN
STEEN GELEYT

Foundation stone

Groat cupboard

47

into moulds and left in the cheese press (Fig. 32) to squeeze out further moisture. After an hour or two the moulds were removed from the press, salt was added and the cheeses were put on a rack in the stalls to dry. The final products were the famous Edam cheeses.

There were numerous regional markets for dairy produce (the one at Alkmaar is still a tourist attraction) and as early as the seventeenth century great quantities of cheese and butter were being exported to England, France, Spain, Portugal, Italy and the Southern Netherlands, by way of main markets like Amsterdam and Rotterdam.

Tile picture in the living room

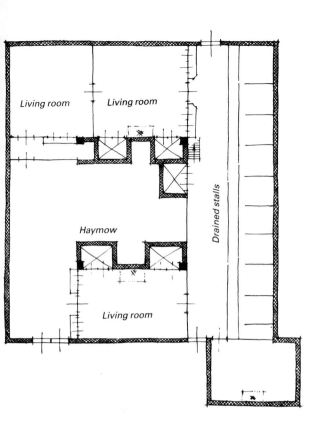

Living room

Living room

Drained stalls

Haymow

Living room

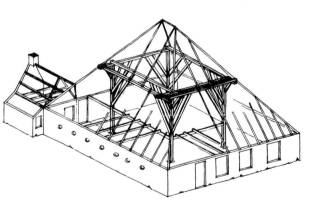

Engraving of a churn-mill

Fig. 1.

BRUGGE tot OUDERKERK.

Ordonnantie van de Ed. Heeren Burgemeesteren en Regeerders der
Stad Amsterdam, achtervolgende 't Octroy by haar Ed. geobtineert van de Ed. Gr. Mog.
Heeren Staaten van Holland en West-Vriesland te betalen, volgens de navolgende
Lyste: te weten, van

Scheepen, Schuyten, Jagten en Pramen met staande Masten -	een stuyver.
Scheepen met leggende Masten	acht penningen.
Schuyten met leggende Masten	vier penningen.
Pramen met leggende Masten	}acht penningen.
Jagten met leggende Masten	
Een Vlor Hout van een Balk langte - - - -	twee stuyvers.
En voorts soo daar meer langten zyn, voor ieder langte	een stuyver.
Ieder overgaande Persoon - - - -	vier penningen.

Uytgesondert een Kind dat noch suygende op den
Arm gedragen werd, zal vry zyn.

Een Wagen met Paarden - - - - -	een stuyver.
Een Geladen Wagen met Goederen en Koopmanschap -	drie stuyvers.
Een Mudde Goeds	vier penningen.
Een Ton Goeds	acht penningen.
Een Koffer	acht penningen.
Een Sleede met Paarden, over en onder	een stuyver.
Een gelade Sleede	drie stuyvers.
Een Paart of Koe-beest - - - - -	acht penningen.
Schapen of Varkens	twee penningen.

Yder Huysgesin van binnen en buyten Bullewijsk / mitsgaders de Waber aan beside zijden ban 't Water / en
den geheelen ronde Hoep / boor overloopen soo beel haar eygen Waaren en Goet bedraagt / sullen geeben twee
schellingen / maar ban ryden en jagen ban anderen / baar mede sy gelt berdienen / sullen sy betalen insgelijks
anderen / als booten.

Alle Schippers die komen zeylen / sullen gehouden wesen haar Zeylen boor de Wind te strykien / ende boorts
alle ende eenen ngelijk / die Col schuldig is / sullen haar geld moeten in de hand hebben / ende betalen.

Ende wanneer twee Scheepen of Schuyten malkanderen in de Brug gemoeten / soo sal den genen / die tegen
de Wind komt / moeten ophouden / tot de andere / die boor de Wind komt / boor de Brug is.

Op pene ban drie Guldens te berbeuren by d'onwillige / d'eene helft ten behoeve ban de Brugman / en de andere
helft ten behoeve ban den Officier die de bekeuringe boen sal.

In kennisse van my Secretaris

WILLEM HUYDECOPER

Te Amsterdam, by PIETER MORTIER, Stads-Drukker en Boekverkoper, in de Warmoesstraat, Oostzyde, het 2de huis
benoorden de St. Anna-straat. *Mei Privilegie*, 1773.

*Toll rates for the double drawbridge from Ouderkerk aan de Amstel,
1773 (33)*

33 Double drawbridge, Ouderkerk aan de Amstel (N.H.)

This bridge was set up in the museum as an example of the design of a moveable cross-river connection. In fact it consists of two lift or balancing bridges, which in the lowered position lean slightly slanting against each other. Each half is composed of a portal arch, the 'hamei', with on it a moveable counterpoise (called the bascule) and a roadway.

The portal arch, made mostly of oak, is supported by one or (such as here) two iron rails against each upright. The round supports between the uprights serve to prevent them tilting sidewards. On the portal arch there is a beam, the head beam. On this there are horizontal iron hinges attached on which the bascule moves. The bascule consists of two tensible pine beams between which a heavy connecting beam is attached at one end. This serves as a counterweight for the roadway, which is connected by chains to the other end of the bascule beams. In some cases the counterweight of the bridge consisted of an open container in which stones provided the weight. The length of the roadway was limited by the weight which could be lifted up by the counterweight. For this reason short or long permanent ramps were necessary on both sides of the bridge at wide stretches of water.

Next to the bridge in the water on both sides of the channel are heavy wooden posts with horizontal beams, serving as restraints to direct the boats through the channel opening and in this way as far as possible to limit damage caused by collisions.

Drawbridges have been used for centuries in The Netherlands to permit the passage of loaded ships or ships with high rigging. In the last century iron constructions gradually took over from drawbridges. In 1939 the bridge at Ouderkerk was replaced by a concrete vertical lift bridge. Then, also the pavement where the washing was done and the bridgeman's wooden shelter, were dismantled.

34 Merchant's house, Koog aan de Zaan (N.H.)

Type of residence of well-to-do merchants and entrepeneurs in the Zaan area.
Behind the façades, which are partly of brick, is a house built virtually entirely of wood, which consists of several wings. The oldest part of it, dating from 1686, is not

Chair

Fireplace

open to the public. In 1740 this was extended by a wing along the street and around 1770 a third wing was built on at rights-angles to the street and the whole building was modernized in accordance with contemporary taste, acquiring outside walls partly of brick and wooden gables with crests and other carving. Later on the street doors were replaced by the present ones. Thus this merchant's house grew into a building of a U-shaped plan round a central courtyard – the 'back yard' as it was called – which in its original situation, as on its present site in the museum, looked out over water, i.e. over the river Zaan, a waterway of the greatest importance to the old industrial area of North Holland.

The interior is mainly installed in accordance with the taste of the well-to-do bourgeoisie in the middle of the 19th century. This naturally tells most strongly in the drawing-room. Older pieces of furniture, which did not fit in with the new modes, were removed from there to less important rooms. So it was that the beautifully painted 'Assendelft' sideboard, dating from about 1700, was banished to the counting-house.

The first room on the right as one goes through the door of the house, was the counting-house. There the mer-

Wall tile

54

chant did his extensive book-keeping. The Zaan merchants had fingers in numerous pies, including the timber trade and sawmilling, ship-building, oil-milling and the oil trade, papermaking, whaling, sailmaking, paint manufacture, the fur trade and baking (ship's biscuits). Behind the counting-house is a kitchen, with a typical North-Holland chimney-piece faced with the tiles painted with Biblical subjects, which were produced in large quantities at that period. Next to this is a partitioned-off section with a cupboard bed. Here one can clearly see the way the house is constructed, with load-bearing posts, beams and panelling all in wood and only the fireplace and chimney flue in brick.

At the back of this wing is a sun parlour. Every merchant's house had a room like this, preferably overlooking the Zaan. It is a sort of conservatory with numerous windows, where people could take coffee or tea in moments of leisure. Here the men smoked their long clay pipes and enjoyed a drink and the women sat over their fancy-work. Sometimes the master of the house would also keep his collection of scientific apparatus here, such as machines for producing electricity, etc. Round games were also played here, but what people particularly enjoyed was watching the busy traffic of the boats on the river Zaan.

In the front room – the salon or 'best end' as it was called in old Zaan parlance – we find furniture and decoration from the middle of the last century.

Clock from the Zaan area

35 Tradesman's house, Zaandam (N.H.)

When it was placed in the museum, this building consisted of two premises: a middle class dwelling and business premises.

The dwelling, with a facade dating from about 1835, originally came from Zaandam (Westzijde, on the corner of the Heeregracht). It is furnished as a shop, the fittings of the shop interior are taken from the museum's own collection. Looking from the entrance, to the right there is a cabinet dating from about 1840, and to the left a cabinet from around the turn of the century. The remainder of the interior is reconstructed following documentation on the Zaan area, available from the museum's collection.

The business premises from Koog aan de Zaan (Zuideinde, on the corner of Breedweer) was built in 1826. A forge was located there. Premises such as this were often to be found in the Zaan area. They housed among other things corn chandler's shops, sailmaker's, and sack making businesses. Characteristic are the hatches high up the side wall. In the open position they ensured that the smoke could disappear without people on the shop floor being affected by the draught.

The museum shop is accommodated in these premises.

36   Garden, Zaan area (N.H.)

Opposite the merchant's house is the garden of pleas-
ance, with a parterre of 'embroidery': clipped hedges
and patterns in grass and in the centre a sundial
surrounded by beds with glass beads laid out in designs.
These beads were mainly made in glass factories in
Amsterdam in the seventeenth and eighteenth centuries
to the commission of the Dutch East and West India
Companies, who used them for trading in the tropics. At
home a use was found for them in laying out small
gardens in place of tropical shells, which were also very
expensive at that time.

The designs in which the beads are laid out feature the
arms of Smit en Honig, those of the couple who lived in
the merchant's house in the first half of the 19th century,
along with those of their mothers, De Jager and Appel,
and some flower motifs. Round about lie beds of flowers
and vegetables. Normally such gardens were much
larger, up to 3000-7000 square metres, but there did also
exist small ones like this, which is only 225 square
metres. Obviously lacking here are the hotbeds and cold
frames, the orchard and the park. To protect the plants
from the wind a garden like this would be surrounded by
a fence, which here makes a fine background with a
summer-house.

Reserve numbers 37 and 38

39 Labourer's house, Zaan area (N.H.)

This very small house belonged to the complex of comfortable living owned by the merchant from Koog aan de Zaan, who rented it to a working class family. The house, with a roof sloping one way, consists of a single room with a cupboard and a cupboard bed, a tiny porch that also served as a kitchen, and a minute attic.

At the beginning of the century, for a house like this working people had to pay about ƒ 1,50 a week, out of wages that were rarely higher than ƒ 5,00 a week. The inhabitants of such a place, mainly elderly couples with married children, nonetheless somehow managed to save a little!

40 Coach-house, Zaan area (N.H.)

This wooden building is an example of a coach-house of the first quarter of the nineteenth century. In it is housed the merchant's carriage and here too were stored in summer the sleigh and ice boat, the status symbols of the rich merchants of those days.

41 Three shop interiors

Three shop interiors are set up in this building: a barber's, a grocer's, and a druggist. The building itself is inspired after a complex lost in a fire at the museum in 1970, that was made up from components from premises from Koog aan de Zaan, the vicarage from Landsmeer and the facade of a building from Krommenie. The current building is representative of the style in the Zaan area in the nineteenth century. All three of the businesses belong to a calling with a medical origin.

Up to the end of the eighteenth century the barber practised elementary medicine alongside cutting and shaving. From the nineteenth century medicine completely became the province of the doctor, while the barber limited himself to cutting, shaving, and personal hygiene.

The men's hairdresser's H. Kippersluijs from Utrecht, belonged to a hairdresser or barber who during three consecutive generations attempted in vain to work his way up to become a 'coiffeur': a barber for well-to-do citizens. The dressing table without washing bowls, the two barber's chairs and the high chair all date from 1890. Since then the inventory had scarcely changed up to 1974, when the business ceased trading.

The grocer, the druggist, and the dispensing chemist were until circa 1600 still united in one trade: the 'kruidenier'. After 1600 the dispensing chemists set themselves apart as belonging to the medical profession in order to specialise in the preparation and sale of compound medicines or composita on doctor's prescription. Around the same time the druggists came up as traders in herbs and basic medicines or simplicia, while the grocers concentrated themselves on spices and subtropical fruits, with coffee and tea as specialities. Under the influence of the industrialisation of foodstuff production and the rise of the brand name, a new type of foodstuffs trader sprang up around 1900, who drove out the specialised grocer. The shop interior of A.J. Hermsen from Renkum is an example of this new type of business. It has the dimensions of a corner shop. The shop was combined with a cafe and after the opening in 1919 changed little until it closed in 1978.

The emergence of patent medicines through the growth of the pharmaceutical industry, the increased demand for nursing requisites for the sick as a result of more intensive health care, and the increased demand for chemicals through technical progress, led to the emergence of a new type of druggist at the end of the nineteenth century.

The druggist's interior in art nouveau style by the architect H.J. Jesse from Leiden, comes from the large town druggist's C. Christiaanse in Leiden and dates from 1909. It sold drugs, poisonous and corrosive substances, chemicals, bandages, patent medicines, perfumes, paints, inflamable and volatile substances, mineral waters and so forth. Because after 1950 the business failed to keep up with modern developments which concentrated on packaged brand names and cosmetics, the interior remained unchanged until the business closed in 1961.

42 Boatyard, Marken (N.H.)

Workshop dating from 1885 with a slipway, for the repair of fishing boats. The boats from Marken were built elsewhere, but the inhabitants maintained them on the sland itself, in the boatyard known as 'De Hoop' which has now come to the museum. Here there is a wooden capstan for hauling the boats up out of the water and a workshop which is built of wood like the cottages and has a raised floor to escape flooding. In the workshop is a collection of shipwright's tools.

At the original location, c. 1943

Pot hanger

43 Fisherman's cottage, Marken (N.H.)

This cottage, like all the cottages on the island of Marken in the Zuyder Zee (now the IJsselmeer), is entirely of wood. It probably dates from c. 1750 and was built on an artificial mound as a safeguard against the floods which were a constant menace before the advent of the enclosing dike. Immediately inside the front door there is a butt in which rainwater from the roof was collected for use as drinking water. There are only two rooms, a small 'best room' and a large living room, which has a wooden partition, or speer, by the front door to prevent the draught reaching the fireplace. Instead of a chimney to take the smoke away there is a wooden shutter in the roof, which can be opened and closed from below by means of a rope. The most striking feature of the interior is the superabundance of ornaments which are heaped or hung up in every available space.

They include plates, which generally have a hole bored in them so that they can be suspended by means of a cord made fast with a wooden toggle or a knot, and numerous pictures of members of the House of Orange (the inhabitants of Marken being nothing if not royalists).

The cupboard beds were not only places to sleep in but played an important part in the decoration of the interior, being made up for show in the daytime, in accordance with a custom that was not exclusive to Marken but was common all over the north-eastern part of the country. Painted furniture and other objects, which were as popular in Marken as they were in Hindeloopen, were generally imported from elsewhere. Oval chip boxes, for instance, came from Germany. A notably seamanlike feature of this interior is the adjustable pot hanger made of cord threaded through a block of wood with two holes in it.

For all their charm these cottages had their drawbacks. The absence of a chimney and of any sanitary arrangements can scarcely have been beneficial to health. At all events they have been blamed for the high death-rate from tuberculosis among the island's population and for their poor resistance to disease.

In the late Middle Ages, when the island was larger than it is now and formed part of the mainland, cattle farming was the main means of subsistance but later on, probably as a result of the erosion of the boggy soil in storms and gales, it became virtually impossible to keep this up on a viable scale and people turned to the sea for their livelihood. In the seventeenth and eighteenth centuries they engaged in whaling in Scandinavian waters and herring fishing round the Dogger Bank. This brought them a certain prosperity which found expression in the 'best rooms', the treasures of which included souvenirs

Clog

Chip box

Ship in a bottle

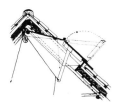

Smoke shutter open and closed

brought back from Scandinavia, Scotland and England. In the nineteenth century whaling declined in importance and competition from other fishing-villages made the herring fishery less lucrative and so they took to fishing nearer home in the Zuyder Zee, exchanging their North Sea boats for craft more suited to shallower waters.

Method of hanging a plate, back and front

63

Chatelaine bag, West-Friesland, 1807

Cupboard bed with embroidered cushions, Marken

44 Sheepcote, Texel (N.H.)

The island of Texel has always been famous for its sheep (wool!). At night time the sheep would be kept in cotes like this one, in which hay was also stored. This cote was probably built before 1800. It is really nothing more than a pyramidical structure cut through the middle, with a central hay-mow around which the sheep were accommodated (32).

Plan and elevations of sheepcote from Texel

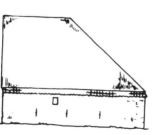

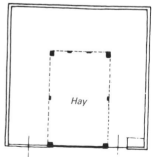

Hay

45 Small drainage mill, Gouda (Z.H.)

Until 1946 this small pasture mill stood between the Old and the New Gouwe below Gouda. It served to drain off several decimetres of water from a ditch, as a result of which the adjoining arable or pasture land could be used. In 1946 the mill was purchased by the museum and brought here.

This type of mill was first used in 1842 at the river Zaan. The length of the sails varies between three and five metres, depending on the size of the area to be drained. A fantail on the moveable body of the mill ensures that the sails automatically face into the wind. When there is little wind planks are fastened on to the sails. The pivot drives the impeller of a simple centrifugal pump. The pump is situated totally under water. The water flowing in next to the pivot is thrust outside by the rotating blades and drains off via an outlet in the pumphouse. A flap prevents the water from flowing back.

46 Fisherman's shack, Amsterdam-North (N.H.)

This shack for one person was part of a collection of about thirty fisherman's shacks, which prior to 1918 stood on the North bank of the IJ. Pedlars of eel and fishmongers from Volendam spent the night there, after they had been peddling their wares at Amsterdam during the day. Sundays were spent with their families in Volendam.

The shacks were mainly made of wood. The walls consisted of a panelling of planks, which were tarred on the outside. The roofs were covered with red tiles or with tarred tarpaulin. Behind the chimney was a cupboard bed with two small cupboards under the bedboards. There was no furniture. One squatted or sat with crossed legs on the floor. On the basis of the Housing Law of 1902 Amsterdam Council declared these dwellings without sanitation uninhabitable.

In 1918 there were only two fisherman's shacks still surviving. The shack which according to tradition had been lived in for sixty-six years by the then aged Gerrit Valk, was purchased by Amsterdam Council and given to the museum. The household effects consisted of: a fireplace (with hearth plate), a trivet, a ship's clock, an iron pot, a kettle for boiling water, a kettle for making coffee, a breadbox, a straw mattress with four blankets, an earthenware butter crock (a Cologne pot), two crucifixes, a fishing boat light, a fork, two spoons, a soldier's soup cauldron, and a mirror. On the wooden floor there was a sail cloth and a small mat. During the second world war this inventory was lost.

The original shack dates from around 1852. From old photographs it is evident, that in the past the front of the building used to have horizontal panelling made of tarred planks with a flattened off gable. Between 1913 and 1918 the front of the building acquired a different appearance, as a result of new woodwork being put on over the panelling.

After the shack was transferred to the museum in 1918, it was, on account of its dilapidated condition, thoroughly repaired in 1928 and in 1981 underwent a total reconstruction. The measurements are: length 3.20 metres, width 2.20 metres, and height 1.85 metres.

At the original location, c. 1913

47 Sawmill, Numansdorp (Z.H.)

This type of windmill – a Dutch invention dating from about 1600 – was specifically designed to saw imported logs into planks and ribs for building ships, houses, etc. The oldest parts of this particular mill, which is a fairly small example, probably date from about 1700. It was originally erected in Dordrecht but in 1854 it was moved to Numansdorp, where it remained in operation until it was brought to the museum. The moving of wooden mills and other wooden structures from one place to another used to be quite common.

The mill can only be viewed from the outside.

Essentially the equipment consists of three saws mounted in vertical frames which were moved up and down by means of a crankshaft installed just below the windshaft (i.e. the axle of the sails). On the workfloor are a series of sledges, each of which held a log in position against the blade of one of the saws and carried it forward a step every time the saw was pulled upwards, so that the next downward stroke would bite into the wood again. To turn the sails into the wind, a winch was used to wind the whole body round, as in the case of the post mill (55). In Dutch a mill like this is called a paltrok, which literally means a smock, but this should not be confused with the English name, smock mill, which is a wooden version of a tower mill, where only the cap is turned.

The idea of the sawmill soon caught on. Medieval methods, using a long two-handed saw over a saw pit were far too slow to keep up with the increasing demand; so it is not surprising that there was a rush to invest in the new invention, even if it did mean an enormous capital outlay. As for the siting of the new mills, it must be remembered that the wood was largely pine and fir from the Baltic and was imported in cargo-boats based on ports like Hindeloopen (which partly owed its prosperity to the trade). Consequently, access to water was needed not only for steeping the new wood but also for reasons of transport; so the mills tended to be concentrated in areas with large tracts of water, like Amsterdam, the Zaan area to the north, and Dordrecht in the south, which were also old-established shipbuilding centres. Here they took their place amongst the hundred of other industrial windmills (for paint, paper, tobacco, spices, oil, etc.) that came to be such a feature of this part of the country in the seventeenth and eighteenth centuries. In the following century however, the picture changed completely. Many of the mills went over to steam and some eventually expanded into large modern concerns. But there were many others that went out of business.

Cross-section through mill

The most important buildings attached to a sawmill were the drying-sheds, where cut timber was left to dry, sometimes for years. There is one of these sheds in the museum (126).

A fair-sized mill will have been run by a master, a foreman, a journeyman and several apprentices. In the 'good old days', with a favourable wind, these will have worked all the hours there were, staying on after dark in wintertime and even sending one of the apprentices round the houses to collect their food so that they did not have to knock off for meals. Under these conditions, if they worked from five in the morning to eight or ten at night, eighty or so logs five to six metres long could probably have been reduced to planks.

48 Drainage mill, Noordlaren (Gr.)

Built around 1862 in order to keep a polder dry. The principle of this drainage mill is the same as the hollow post mill (118). Here again it is a screw which hauls up the water, but the housing and winding mechanism are different. It is in fact a wooden version of a tower mill (90), known as a smock mill. In this particular instance, the wooden boards which line the tapering octagonal framework are thatched over, and so is the rotatable cap. It is capable of drawing up to 50 or 60 cubic metres of water a minute and is a fine example of drainage mill design of the type perfected by the Dutch by about 1650. *The mill can only be viewed from the outside.*

The windmill as such is not a Dutch invention and did not really begin to take a hold until about 1100. The earliest types were post mills for grinding corn (97), and it seems that the earliest drainage mills also evolved from the post mill, possibly about 1400. Before then the low-lying areas in the north and west of the country had been continually affected by floods, which washed away large tracts of land. But after the first major attempts at building up the coastal defences at the beginning of the fourteenth century, it was possible to start reclaiming land by draining the lakes and meres. The first mills to work at all satisfactorily under these conditions were rather like the hollow post mills, though perhaps slightly larger and with paddle or bucket wheels instead of screws. With these considerable expertise and know-how were built up and eventually this led to a period of intense activity between 1575 and 1650, when the great drainage mills of Holland were developed. Two engineers whose names are closely associated with this development were Jan Adriaansz. Leeghwater and Simon Stevin. But knowhow alone was not enough, of course. Capital and enormous enterprise were needed — and also available. To quote one example, reclamation of the Schermerpolder in North Holland, which was begun in 1631, needed 51 large mills drawing a total of 1000 cubic metres of water a minute over a period of four years before the ground was dry enough to be worked.

One of the problems with drainage mills is that their lifting power is limited, i.e. they cannot lift water above a certain height. To drain a lake and keep it dry, it was often necessary to raise the water up to four or five

metres, which meant that a number of mills working in series had to be used. The diagram below shows how a series of three such mills with paddle wheels might operate. After 1650 the paddle wheel was gradually ousted in North Holland, Friesland and Groningen by the screw, and by the beginning of the nineteenth century steam pumps began to make their appearance; but it was still a long time before the highly efficient windmill was finally made redundant. The one in the museum, dating from 1862, is still exactly like the seventeenth-century mills, with only a few minor concessions to the 'modern' steam age, such as a cast-iron windshaft for the sails.

It is difficult to appreciate the effect drainage mills have had on the appearance and agricultural economy of the western and northern parts of the country since 1600. Large lakes have been turned into rich farmland, boggy moorland has been turned into meadows, and meadows have been converted, by even better drainage, into highly profitable arable land. The reasons for this development were partly connected with the general expansion of trade and shipping and with the rising demand for raw materials by the new industrial mills that were going up in the west. As a result the farmers in the region acquired a modern approach to farming much sooner than their counterparts elsewhere (cf. 23,

Drainage in steps

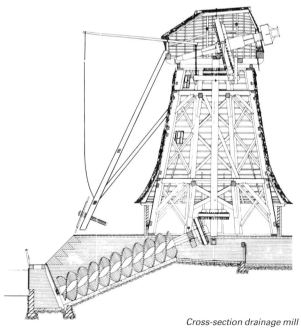

Cross-section drainage mill

32, 78): they were exploiting the land to satisfy national and international markets and were therefore only too ready to invest in dikes and drainage schemes. However, careful planning was also needed and this was put in the hands of specially instituted regional boards with very wide powers of control over dikes and bridges as well as waterways and drainage. For it was obvious that although dependence on the voluntary help of one's neighbours worked well on a small scale in villages and hamlets, this was not enough when it came to safeguarding extensive tracts of fertile polder, sometimes several metres below sea level.

Reserve numbers 49-54

55 Post mill, Huizen (N.H.)

In a post mill all the machinery is housed in an upright wooden body (the buck) which stands and pivots on a

hefty wooden **post** (hence the name). Some of the thrust of the wind, however, is also taken by the tail which consists of steps and a pole (tail pole) for turning the whole mill round. This particular example, which is smaller than most, was used to grind corn. A hoist for rainsing sacks of corn and meal can be seen under the small hood above the gallery at the back. This was driven from the shaft connected to the sails. The millstones in the buck itself are encased in a wooden tun into which the grain was fed from a hopper with a tapered shoe and from which the meal ran down through a trough or spout into sacks. Many parts of this mill are two to three hundred years old. In 1976 the mill underwent a thorough renovation.
It is only to be viewed from the outside.

Post mills were common all over the Low Countries as

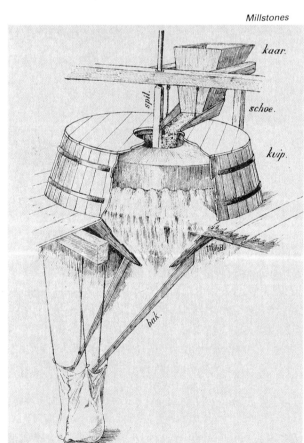

Millstones

kaar.

spil.

schoe.

kuip.

bak.

far back as the middle ages. They are often depicted in medieval miniatures and are an interesting example of the way medieval builders thought in wood, which they used for everything, including the roof and moving parts like shafts and cogwheels. It is also typical that the only method they had of getting the sails to face square into the wind was to turn the whole buck on its post. This process was called **winding** and was done by using the winch on the tail to wind-in a rope or chain that had been hitched to one of a series of low posts set in a circle round the mill.

At a period when wind and water were the only other sources of energy apart from men and animals, no-one was allowed to build or operate a mill without first having purchased the franchise to use this energy from the lord of the manor or other relevant authority. The landowner, however, could build a mill himself, in which case he would usually lease it to a miller, and he also possessed what were known as 'soke rights', whereby he could compel all those living in the area to have their corn ground at his mill and no-one else's. Manorial franchises like this were eventually abolished by Napoleon about 1800, but the old system of paying the miller with scoops of corn he had ground, which he could then sell, did not die out altogether for another hundred years.

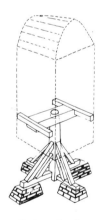

Post construction

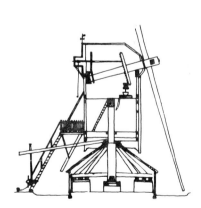

Cross-section of a post mill

56 Laundry, Overveen (N.H.)

These brick buildings were originally laid out, perhaps before 1700, as a bleachery. After various alterations, however, particularly after 1800, it was eventually converted into a laundry, where better-off families from Amsterdam and thereabouts used to send their linen to be done once or twice a year. The equipment includes a boiler with hot water tank, a copper (for boiling the wash), large tubs sunk into the floor (for soaking and rinsing) and an impressive horse-mill-type system for pounding the linen in the baths of warm suds. The pounders worked off the huge camshaft which runs above the beams to the gearing connected to the actual horse-driven shaft. They were essentially a mechanized form of the tub and dolly 'which grandmother used' and a forerunner of the first wooden washing machines.

Mangle

After being washed, the linen was bleached and then finished off in a mangle. In the nineteenth century bleaching was still done by spreading the washing out in the sun on what was known as the bleaching ground. The mangles in this laundry consist of wooden rollers pressed down and rotated by a heavily weighted wooden casing which is wound back and forth. The buildings are in three parallel and adjoining sections, part of which (not open to the public) used to be lived in by the owner of the bleachery. The small bay built on at the front served as a lookout to guard against any thieving from the bleaching ground.

Though in our eyes these buildings may seem rather domestic and picturesque, they are in fact an important industrial monument: a reminder of the famous linen bleacheries of Kennemerland that commanded such a high reputation throughout Europe in the sixteenth and seventeenth centuries. Kennemerland is a sand-dune area to the north of Haarlem and the excellence of its bleacheries was due to the purity of the water from the dunes. Their existence was one of the reasons why linen weaving in Haarlem began to develop into an important export industry from about 1500 on. This trade was boosted even further by the influx of Flemish weavers, bleachers and textile merchants after 1580, as well as by the enormous expansion in Dutch foreign trade in general around 1600. The Flemings, who were driven north by the continuing war with Spain and growing religious persecution, brought with them considerable expertise, while the significance of foreign trade can be judged from the fact that as early as 1590 there appear to have been merchants from Haarlem and Amsterdam living in Poland, where much of the linen thread came from (flax spinning having greatly expanded as a rural industry in Silesia in the sixteenth century, however poorly paid). Also, The Netherlands used to be the international trading centre for Baltic potash, which was a major raw material in the bleaching process, being lixiviated to a lye and neutralized with sour milk, of which there was a plentiful supply from the dairy farms of North Holland.
By the beginning of the seventeenth century the industry was at its height and the bleacheries were treating

Handbarrow

not only local linen but also cloth imported from Flanders, Westphalia and France; this was then exported again to England, France, Portugal and Spain as 'Holland', 'toile de Hollande', etc., thus providing a good example of an international trade cycle with, typically, the Dutch trader and entrepreneur at the centre. At this period in fact there were as many as twenty large establishments in the area, each employing 40 to 60 people, as well as a dozen or so smaller places. Many of the workers were women and many were migrants from places like Westphalia, Münsterland and Brabant, who flocked to Kennemerland in their hundreds in the spring at the start of the bleaching season. The pay was poor by local standards and the conditions in the bleaching works, which used a lot of chemicals and thus caused considerable water pollution, were not attractive.

By about 1650, however, the whole of the linen industry round Haarlem had already begun to decline, being siphoned away into the countryside where lower wages prevailed. The bleacheries still managed to keep going, particularly those producing better quality material, but with the establishment of new bleaching agents based on chlorine at the beginning of the nineteenth century, even they were forced to give up and move over to laundering.

Truck

At the original location, c. 1930

At the original location, c. 1930

Laundry in its original surroundings, 1864

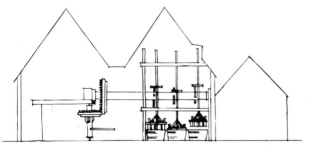

Pounder mechanism

Laundry lists

81

57 Commoner's cottage, Bedum (Gr.)

A simple building dating from around 1850, which was characteristic for the area around the city of Groningen. Cottages of this type, with a small stall, were frequently built around the city to accomodate working and lower middle class families. This type of house was also common along the waterways associated with 'peat colonies'. Sometimes they were on a somewhat larger scale (crofters). The relatively large red brick is characteristic of this area. The toll collector's house from Zuidlaren (113) belongs likewise to this type.

Interior of C. Christiaanse's druggist shop from Leiden (41)

58 Outhouse, 't Woold (Gld.)

This small building from the Achterhoek has two hand-looms set up with their appurtenances.

59-61 Workmen's cottages, Tilburg (N.B.)

In the nineteenth century Tilburg developed itself into an industrial town with a village outlook. The wool industry had already existed in the area for centuries. It was previously carried out as a cottage industry and subsequently became concentrated in factories with steam machines providing the driving force. A great demand for houses was created by the need to house workers. The terrain belonging to the council was so large, that it was not necessary to resort to tenement blocks. On the contrary, following local tradition modest terrace houses were built.

The three houses in the museum date from the second half of the nineteenth century. The largest corner house on the left included originally a room in which a loom was set up in front of the window at the back. The other two houses each have an entrance hall and a room at the back, which served as a kitchen. In the rooms there were cupboard beds. Underneath one of these a cellar was dug out.

The reconstruction of the workmen's cottages in the museum was undertaken in 1957-58, according to a museological concept.

The houses are used for museum services.

62 Clogmaker's workshop

This workshop shows the traditional arrangement of tools and equipment used by a clogmaker, or clogger, until quite recently. The village clogmaker would make clogs to measure, taking account of his customers' requirements and the peculiarities of their feet. In the nineteenth century, however, there was also a highly developed cottage industry engaged in mass-producing clogs, albeit by hand, for people in the towns, where they were particularly popular among the working classes. In the village of Enter in Overijssel, for example, practically the whole working population was occupied in supplying clogs to dealers, who sent them to all parts of the country. As with other cottage industries the money earned in this way was by no means sufficient to meet the needs of the household and consequently a certain amount of farming was carried on as well, mainly by the women.

Clogs were mostly made from poplar or willow which, after being sawn into logs of the required length, was split into wedge-shaped billets. The billet was then shaped by axe and adze into a rough clog which was fined down on the bench with a clogger's knife. After this the clogs were firmly clamped down in pairs on

Axe

Saw

87

Adze

Hollowing-out bench

another bench and hollowed out with special gouges and knives. A skilled clogger could get up to 50 pairs out of a cubic metre of wood and, by working from six in the morning to seven in the evening, could make an average of ten pairs a day. Around 1910 a village clogmaker, working in this way, would have earned ƒ 10,00 a week, which was fairly reasonable, but things were not nearly so favourable in the cottage industry. Anyone making clogs for a dealer could not expect to get much above 13 cents a pair, which meant he could scarcely earn ƒ 1,50 a day, and this at a time when the weekly food bill alone (excluding meat) for a man with a wife and a child of four would have been at least ƒ 5,50. 'It is a wonder the inhabitants have not died out', commented a writer of the period on the village of Enter, and things were not much better elsewhere, though the price paid per pair may have been a cent or two higher. In fact it was probably only by cultivating their little patches of land, and keeping a few pigs, goats and perhaps a cow, that most people did manage to survive.

If an assistant was employed, he would get the same rate for the job as his master got from the dealer, but on the other hand it was left to him to do the heavier work of hollowing the clogs out, which took about 45 minutes per pair as against 20 minutes for the initial roughing out and 10 for the final shaping.

The workshops were generally stuffy, damp and dark as well as pokey. Many clogmakers, however, did not have a separate workshop and had to use the living-room,

Roughed-out clog

Clog maker in Lieshout (N.B.), 1949

Clogmaker's knife

which was often the only room in the house. And as if all this was not bad enough they were also up against strong competition from other people who were prepared to work for even less than they were, as is evident from the fact that between 1910 and 1915 imports of clogs from Belgium amounted to an average of 2½ million kilogrammes a year (a large pair of man's clogs weighing about one kilogramme.)

Billet

Much the same sort of picture could be painted of any of the cottage handwork industries around the turn of the century. Whatever the innumerable workers employed in this way produced, whether it was shoes, nails, fastenings or cigars, they were all condemned to lead a thoroughly miserable existence.

Literature: H. Noorlander, Wooden shoes, their makers and their wearers, 1978 (available in museum shop and kiosk).

63 Farm labourer's cottages, Zandeweer (Gr.)

This cottage, dating from about 1850, was transferred to the museum in 1957 and fitted up as a forge.

64 Shoeing-shed, Scherpenzeel (N.H.)

A shoeing-shed belonged to a blacksmith's or an ordinary forge in which horses were shod. The Dutch name for this: 'travalje' comes from the Middle Dutch word 'travaelge', which in turn is derived from the Latin 'trepalium', a tool of turture consisting of three beams. Shoeing-sheds were either inside the smithy's itself or just outside, with or without a shelter.
This shoeing-shed was purchased in 1923 and rebuilt in the museum in 1925. It can accomodate two horses.

65 Farm labourer's cottage, Beemster (N.H.)

Only to be viewed from the outside.

Skeleton of a farm from Vragender (Gld.) (130)

66 Weighbridge and weighhouse, Wolphaartsdijk (Zld.)

Virtually every village had a weighbridge in the past. Carts laden with farm produce ran from the roadway on to the platform of the weighbridge, where they were weighed contents and all. The weighing mechanism was installed in the weighhouse and there the weights were read off and written down on chits, which had to be handed in when the farmers were paid for their produce by their customers.

The weighbridge on Veerweg at Wolphaartsdijk was in use from around 1933 to 1960, mainly for weighing sugar beet or sugar-beet pulp and potatoes. The laden carts were weighed on their way to the harbour there, before being carried further on barges. In the course of the sixties barges were superseded by lorries as the means of transport, so that the weighbridge gradually passed out of use. Weighbridges still play an important role, however, but nowadays they are much bigger and have electrical or automated weighing mechanisms.

The Wolphaartsdijk weighbridge and weighhouse belonged to 'Eendracht', the local weighbridge association. The sort of things that used to be weighed on it can be seen from a scale of charges of 1954. The weighing machine is of a kind with a rod system, a type of scale in common use in the thirties. Part of it is in the weighhouse, the rest under the wooden platform in the roadway. The maximum weight it will take is ten tons (ten thousand kilograms). The weigbridge is original, the weighhouse a reconstruction.

67　Commercial depot, Goes (Zld.)

This commercial depot was built beside the railway line at Goes around 1915. It was used by the firm of Massee & Zoon for the storage and distribution of imported agricultural machinery, mainly from Britain and America. The firm sent out brochures to possible buyers and also held regular viewing days for them. There was a small sales office in the depot and assembly work was probably done there too.

The supporting construction of the roof is a mixture of traditional and modern building methods. Wooden posts are used as in the traditional transverse frame (103). These are placed against the brick buttresses of the wall, posts and buttresses between them supporting the roof. The roof construction is also of wood, but because of the large size of the span, it has iron tie rods. In this construction, which enables large areas to be spanned, the support of wooden posts is actually superfluous.

Inside the building are displayed a number of larger examples of agricultural implements and means of transport from the museum's collection.

Reserve numbers 68-71

72 Herb garden

In a variety of ways herbs have always played an important role in the life of man. The arrangement of the herb garden in the museum corresponds to an old Dutch herb garden and provides information about the use of herbs in medicine, in the home, and in handicrafts and industry (such as the herbs from which dyes and oil are derived). A part of the garden accomodates a collection of plants which have played a role in religion and superstition, the so called 'legend plants'. The location of the herb garden is on the site of the vegetable garden of the former estate 'De Waterberg', and it has thus been in cultivation for centuries.

The medicinal herb garden

In the Middle Ages looking after the sick was mainly the job of the monks. This is why in the monasteries the herb garden was mostly next to the accomodation for the sick: the hospice. In the Middle Ages the nobility often had a herb garden for a variety of purposes. Very well known is the decree of Charlemagne (742-814), in which was stipulated what herbs were to be grown in the gardens of his castles. The decree contained a list of more than seventy species.

In the towns, especially after the Reformation, looking after the sick was the responsibility of the town government. This was an important job because of the many epidemics (bubonic plague), caused by poor hygienic conditions. Apothecaries employed by the town, got the opportunity to lay out gardens in or near the town.

Herb garden after 1955

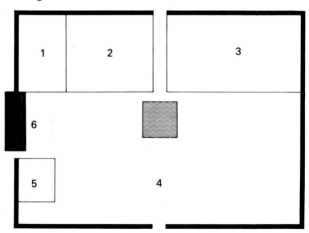

1 Dye plants	4 Medicinal herbs
2 Kitchen herbs	5 Monastery garden
3 Legend herbs	6 Exhibition/Apothecary's workshop

The herb garden in the museum is an example of such an apothecary's garden.

Just as in other gardens we can recognise the different epochs in which the garden was laid out, namely the Middle Ages, the Renaissance, and the Baroque. Characteristic are the medieval wall and the bank made of sods in the garden of Reichenau, the renaissance design of the lay out of the garden, the baroque town pump from Zwolle, and the equally baroque entrance gates. The medicinal herbs are classified in groups according to their use. The groups are separated by small hedges.

The monastery garden

The monastery garden in the medicinal herb garden is a replica of a garden near the monastery of Reichenau, laid out by the abbot Walahfridus Strabo. He describes the garden in detail in a didactic poem of 827. In this appears a good account of the knowledge people at that time had of the garden and plants for the purpose of medicine. Strabo's design for the garden was in its turn a replica of a monastery garden in Sankt-Gallen.

The names of the plants in the museum garden are those of the medieval period. Some of these are still easy to recognise, because part of the medieval name is to be found in the current Latin name. Anthriscus cerefolium (garden chervil) for example was called cerefolium in Middle Ages, and Salvia sclaera (clary) was sclarea. Other names may cause confusion. Gladiola does not stand for our gladiolus, but for Iris germanica, garden iris.

The monastery garden

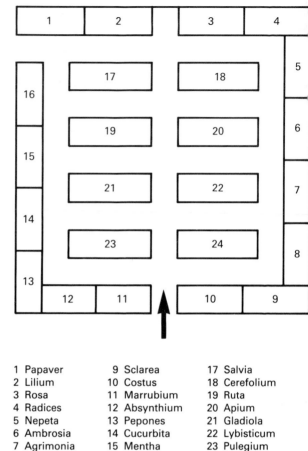

1 Papaver	9 Sclarea	17 Salvia
2 Lilium	10 Costus	18 Cerefolium
3 Rosa	11 Marrubium	19 Ruta
4 Radices	12 Absynthium	20 Apium
5 Nepeta	13 Pepones	21 Gladiola
6 Ambrosia	14 Cucurbita	22 Lybisticum
7 Agrimonia	15 Mentha	23 Pulegium
8 Vetlonica	16 Abrotanum	24 Feniculum

73 Herb garden exhibition room

Exhibitions relating to the herb garden are put together
in this building. It also houses equipment used for treating herbs.

74 'De Hanekamp' inn, Zwolle (Ov.)

For more than two centuries 'De Hanekamp' (The Cockpit) enjoyed an exceptional reputation in Zwolle and a wide area roundabout, not only as an inn, but also as a café and place of recreation. It was built around 1750 and extended in 1840 with a farmhouse section built on at the back with large barn, with stalls for cows and horses. It was conveniently situated just outside the town on the main road to Salland and Twente. Many livestock dealers, after having visited the busy markets in Zwolle, unharnessed their horses there in order to settle their business and spend the night.

The inn has a taproom with an old-fashioned bar and tiled fireplace and, above the cellar vaults, a mezzanine room with cupboard beds. 'De Hanekamp' is open throughout the season as a café for museum visitors.

Pancakes a speciality!

Interior of A. J. Hermsen's grocery from Renkum (41) ▶

75 Village school, Lhee (Dr.)

A rectangular building made of brick on a pebblestone foundation. It probably dates from shortly before 1750 and consists of only one classroom. Inside there are a number of objects that were used in education in former times. In the centre there is an open hearth under a wooden hood. The interior has been arranged to give some idea of what a country school was like and what sort of things would be used in it in the early nineteenth century (1800-30).

The strong sense of community found amongst the people of Drenthe (76) was not only directed towards solving problems specifically connected with farming: more than one village school like this owed its existence to the initiative of local farmers.

Like the shepherd, the teacher was in the service of the community and took his meals with the various farmers turn and turn about. He was, however, a sort of seasonal worker, as there was no school in summer when the children had to help on the land. His salary was minimal and he would have to supplement it by selling such requisites of learning as quill pens, ink, paper and so on. He might also act as sexton or perform some other service such as winding the church clock every day. It was his pupils who supplied the fuel (peat, turves, etc.) for the fire. Needless to say, the education he dispensed

Disgrace mark

Ferule

was not of a very high order, being largely confined to the three R's and religious instruction.

Satchel

76 Farmhouse, Zeijen (Dr.)

Up to about the beginning of this century, this type of farmhouse was common along the sandy ridges stretching southwards from the south-east corner of Groningen to the eastern (Achterhoek) region of Gelderland. Known locally as a **los hoes**, it is characterized by the absence of a dividing wall between the house place (i.e. the farm kitchen and its hearth) and the barn: men and beasts lived together in one large communal area. This particular example from Drenthe has an **aisle on either side of the central nave** and both inside and outside walls are filled in with wattle and daub. The furnishings and fitments, in the style of a large los hoes of around 1700, are based on material found during the demolition of a farmhouse in Zeijen, near Assen.

Compared with 103, the only differences in construction are the addition of the aisles, formed by bringing the roof down beyond the posts, and the omission of the cumbersome curved-tree roof-trusses. The result was a highly compact and efficient design, since the low aisles were quite high enough for stalls while the tall nave would easily take a fully laden farmcart as well as allow for the swinging of flails and sticks when the barn floor was being used as a threshing-floor. The removal of the curved-tree trusses also meant that there was now more storage space in the loft above the beams, which was important because threshing was only done as and when the grain was required, thereby making it necessary to store the harvest for some time in sheaves.

On entering the barn, which faces the road at the front of the building, we find ourselves on the broad, mud **threshing-floor**, with the loft above, and in the aisle on the

Reel

Skep

right the **sunken stall** for the fifteen to twenty head of cattle that would have been kept on a farm of this size. 'Stall' is perhaps a euphemism, as it is really little more than a pit dug in the ground. But, like the other parts of the building, it served its purpose very effectively, allowing the farmer simply to strew the cow-dung with layers of chopped straw and turf, until eventually the animals stood on a level with the floor of the barn. It would then be cleaned out and the manure would be used to enrich the arable land on which the rye, buckwheat and other cereals were grown.

Hackle

The manure, in fact, was the main reason for keeping cows on a farm like this, and the same could often be said of sheep, especially in Drenthe. Unlike cows, however, which consumed some of the farm's cereal produce, sheep were quite content with what they could find on the surrounding heathland, and all that was needed to collect their droppings was to drive them into pens every night. Also, some of the wool they provided could be sold, and some could be spun into yarn to weave cloth for the family's own use.

Indeed, much of what the farm produced went to satisfy the household's own needs, which were quite considerable. Besides wool for clothes, rye was needed to bake bread and quite a sizeable proportion of the produce went as payment in kind to the farm labourers and the craftsmen that had to be called in from time to time. Even so, a large farm like this would usually still have quite a good surplus of grain and wool, which would be sold, often outside the district, to provide money for various 'luxuries' as well as a little capital to put by for hard times or to invest in equipment or perhaps a horse. (Horse trading and rearing were very important in Drenthe.)

Threshing stick

A writer at the beginning of the nineteenth century, commenting on the los hoes, pointed out that the great advantage of this centuries-old method of building was that the woman of the house could sit at her spinning-wheel, keeping an eye not only on the fire, the food in the pot and the baby in the cradle, but also on all the livestock as well as the rest of the family at work in the barn, and could issue her orders without stirring from her chair. Nowadays, however, it is thought that another important reason for this type of design was that the smoke rising freely from the open fire was an excellent means of drying and preserving the harvest stored in the loft.

Steelyard

The land in Drenthe – old and well established though it was – was only partly cultivated and the few villages that there were, scattered about the landscape, were

Flail

fairly small, just a few large farms clustered round a tree-lined green (usually with a pond in the middle) and here and there houses belonging to less well-off small-holders, labourers and village craftsmen. These smaller houses were generally more or less scaled-down versions of the large farmhouses, and although their inhabitants usually had a small piece of land and a few head of cattle, this was not sufficient to live off. Instead they bartered their labour, services and produce for food and the use of capital goods which they could not afford themselves, but which the larger farmers could provide, like horses, ploughs and farm wagons. As a result, the large farmer, smallholder (hardly distinguishable from the farm labourer) and craftsmen, bound by their dependence on one another, came to form a close-knit community in which people lived frugally but generally managed to ward off impoverishment.

Pitchfork

Aisled structure, cross-section

Aisled structure framework

77   Day labourer's hut, Onstwedde (Gr.)

This cabin is little more than a hole in the ground with a roof over it. Roof and walls consist mainly of turves cut from the peat, with some wooden planking on the front wall. Such places were still being built even at the beginning of this century.

Even the simplest of cottages (12) was beyond the reach of the very poorest members of society, and in the peat-soil areas, particularly in Friesland, Groningen and Drenthe, the lowest-paid workers generally had recourse to turf cabins like this. They included peat-cutters and those who worked as casual labourers for farmers who settled on the agricultularly excellent land that was left after the peat had been removed. (It was particularly well suited to the growing of potatoes which, among other things, could be made into potato flour). When there was no other work to be had, they would fall back on making brooms or breaking stones for the roads, and if they were lucky, they might be able to supplement their meagre diet with the produce of a bit of land and a goat. On the older sandy soils of Drenthe, where the poor were generally taken care of by the community (76), there were far fewer of these hovels to be seen. It is quite wrong to suppose that this lamentable state of affairs only came into being in the nineteenth century, for there are indications that large numbers of agricultural labourers were obliged to live in more or less the same way in the seventeenth and eighteenth centuries.

Such poverty-stricken people, however, generally leave little trace behind them. Written or pictorial records are very few and far between and even their dwellings are made of flimsy materials and soon fall into decay. It is not surprising therefore that the example in the museum has to be completely renewed from time to time.

These so called turf cabins existed until around 1900.

78 Farmhouse, Midlum (Fr.)

Gable finial

Prosperous farm, which in this form dates from 1778. The plans of the alterations in this year have remained intact. Farms like this, often characterised as the head, neck and body type, were built as arable and dairy farms on the fertile marine clays in the part of Friesland known as the Bouwhoek, to the north-east of Harlingen. The 'head' is a neat little farmhouse built in exactly the same way as contemporary houses in towns and villages, with a tiled roof and load-bearing brick walls. It contains the parlour, etc. and behind it, in the 'neck' and 'shoulder' of the barn, are the kitchen, churn room and milk cellar. The barn is an enormous aisled structure (76) which was rebuilt in 1778 (the plans for this operation being still extant). In the nave are large mows (22) for hay and cereal crops, with a threshing-floor (5) at the back complete with horse-driven threshing-machine. The aisle leading off the churn room houses a row of drained stalls (5), while the other one, with a large door at either end, serves as a passageway.

Coffee mill

The long barn, with large mows in the centre under a high roof and a pasageway at the side to facilitate stacking is strongly reminiscent of the 'Flemish' barns of North Brabant and Belgium (97). It is quite different in form from the farmbuilding from North Holland (32), which has livingrooms, stalls, etc., grouped round a central square haymow, but research has shown that both types were the result of the same process of evolution which began with a comparatively small structure housing living quarters and stalls, with separate hay barracks (which later developed into separate barns), and ended with a vast building in which everything was brought together under the same roof. This type of farm was common in Friesland in the seventeenth century and was technically very advanced for that period, with a high degree of mechanization: compare the threshing-machine here with the flail at 76, and the churning mechanism, driven by the horse-mill in the barn (visible through the hatch in the churn room), with the hand churn at 115. Butter making, in fact, was an extremely important activity in this area. The first step in the process was to leave the milk in the milk cellar in flat, oval copper pans (creamers) until the cream had come to the top and could be skimmed off. The cream was then put into a **churn** and agitated vigorously with a dasher (a longhandled plunger with holes in it) until it coalesced to form butter. The butter was salted to preserve it and

Muckbarrow

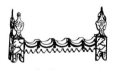

Bucket rack

Rocking-horse

Ornamental bowl

Creamer

Churn

eventually passed into the hands of middlemen to be sold, some of it being exported via Harlingen to countries such as England.

One of the notable things about Dutch agriculture is the contrast between the farms on the older, poorer soils in the east of the country, North Brabant and elsewhere, which were generally small and belonged to the people who worked them, and those on the fertile reclaimed land, which were frequently larger but run by tenants. Thus most of the large farms in Friesland, including this one, belonged to absentee landlords who lived in places like Weesp, Amsterdam, Zeist and Utrecht; and they were well worth having, as their high yields meant one could charge a correspondingly high rent.

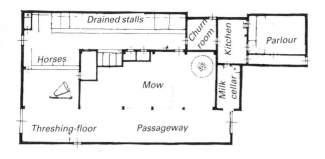

Drained stalls

Churn room

Kitchen

Parlour

Horses

Mow

Milk cellar

Threshing-floor

Passageway

79 Sheepcote, Daarle (Ov.)

See 13.
Only to be viewed from the outside.

80 Farmstead, Beerta (Gr.)

Medium sized farm of the so called 'Oldambtster' type, which in the first half of the eighteenth century began to spread over the south of Groningen (in Westerwolde and the Oldambt, on the denuded land of the peat colonies and further west as far as the Westerkwartier) and the north of Drenthe. On account of the ravages of cattle plague at that time these farms were from the start used mainly for arable purposes. The barns were closely similar to those of Friesland in construction and arrangement (Fig. 78).

This farmhouse, 'Kloostergare' (Cloister Garth), which in its original form dates from 1796, exhibits the transitional stage between the early way of farming, as represented by, for example, the Frisian farm, and more modern methods. This transition, which took place at the beginning of the present century, may be seen in, among other things, the way the buildings have been adapted (e.g. the sloping wall with large doors, calculated to suit the turning-circle of larger mechanized farm machinery) and from changes in the arrangement and installation (in the living-quarters, for instance).

It was at that period that electricity came in as a new source of power. Outside stands a reconstructed overhead supply line, while a radio, electric light, an electric fire and an electric stove form part of the equipment inside.

The living-quarters are decorated and furnished in a manner illustrative of that of the thirties. The furniture in the living-room of the farmhouse was used in that very room around 1935. The built-in wall around the cupboard beds is an older part of the living-room, dating from 1797, when the farmhouse was built. In the thirties some of the beds behind it were converted into cupboards. The modern tiled mantlepieces* are a replacement of the original large open fireplaces. The tiles on the walls disappeared behind wallpaper at the same time.

The farmhouse is, for the rest, fairly soberly appointed, but despite this there certainly existed a measure of prosperity, at any rate for the farmer. The holdings of land gradually became quite large, up to 50 hectares or so, on which were grown wheat, rye, oats and caraway and, from the middle of last century, potatoes for use in distilling and flour-making. Threshing was done in the open part of the barn. In this example the hollowed-out stones in which the pivot for the threshing-machine was placed are still in the floor. In order to allow enough room for the machine to turn round, the heavy supporting posts were placed at an angle at that point.

The farm girls and labourers originally lived with the farmer and his family, but later, as we have seen, they were banished to the back premises, where they had little privacy.

For the rest, the farmer did not own the land but had tenancy rights over it, which dated from the Reformation, when the monastic lands were confiscated by the city of Groningen. Originally there was a tenancy agreement whereby a quit-rent had to be paid by the one side and (should the agreement be ended) compensation by the other for the farmhouse built on the land. In the eighteenth and nineteenth centuries this regulation was changed in such a way that the rent (now a lump sum) became non-withdrawable and 'everlasting' and the land might be bequeathed or transferred to others by the tenant, now a perpetual leaseholder. As a result of this the farmer was in practice virtually able to dispose of the land as if he were the owner.

The similarity between this barn and those of the Frisian farmhouses is no accident, for in fact the barn developed in Friesland was simply taken over in the Oldambster farmhouse and combined with the house part of the older farmhouse with stalls for animals (78). The transition between the two parts is marked by indentations in the side walls. Above the house was added a loft for the storage of threshed grain, which could be reached from the barn.

Originally the house was actually lived in and it was not

until a later period that there came to be living-quarters – and for the hands sleeping-quarters as well – in the barn, while a room at the front was set aside as a show-piece.

* The mantlepieces will be left untiled until the museum has been able to acquire undamaged tiles of the thirties.

Construction

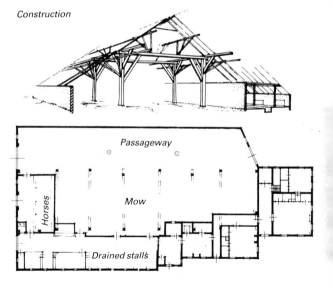

Passageway

Horses

Mow

Drained stalls

Preparation of soil for sowing: from left to right, disc harrow, zig-zag harrow, land roller, Haarlemmermeer, c. 1946

Mechanical reaping of corn with a self-binder, Oosternieland (Gr.), c. 1930

*Sampler, silk thread in cross-stitch on linen. Text: This cloth belongs to
Neeltje Bestebroer (1765-1769)*

*Sampler, silk thread in long armed cross-stitch in linen.
Made by an eleven year old girl. Marken, 1663*

81 T.b. patient's hut, Olst (Ov.)

Thousands of sufferers from T.B. (consumption or tuberculosis) took rest cures in small huts like this from the beginning of this century up to the Second World War. They were isolated in this way in order to reduce the risk of infection. Fresh air and rest assisted recovery and these were often difficult to find in people's homes owing to lack of space and good ventilation.

The huts often stood side by side on the terrain of a public health association building, a field near a village or land belonging to a more isolated farm. They are simple, easily dismountable structures, with as many doors and windows as possible for the admittance of fresh air and light. The whole hut could be rotated according to the direction of the wind and the position of the sun.

Tuberculosis is a dangerous infectious illness, of which many people died until well into this century. Lack of hygiene, bad nutrition and poor housing enabled it to flourish. It was in the cities that the most wretched conditions were to be found and so it was there that the public health associations came into being at the beginning of this century as one of the methods of combatting disease and other evils. Since the emphasis lay on treatment, instruction and assistance for families in their own homes, these associations were encouraged to develop a network of local branches. The movement was funded by collections, government subsidies and subscriptions.

Education and prevention were the main weapons in the fight againt T.B. To this end district nurses were appointed to visit people in their own homes and disinfecting-stations and consultation centres were set up. In order to offer some practical help, the public health associations took to lending out such aids as huts for the patients. Thanks to the massive campaigns for diagnosing it at an early stage by such methods as X-raying, T.B. is no longer a common illness.

Reserve numbers 82-85

86   Parlour, Hindeloopen (Fr.)

This building is not original but the façade gives some idea of the type often found in the little Zuyder Zee port of Hindeloopen in the days when it boasted a considerable population of well-to-do master mariners and other seafaring men. Inside, an attempt has been made, using materials such as tiles, painted furniture and woodwork that are largely authentic, to show what the 'best room' in such a house would have looked like shortly before 1800.

Kettle

The mariners of Hindeloopen owed their prosperity in the seventeenth and eighteenth centuries to the trade they did with Scandinavia and the Baltic countries, carrying goods for the entrepreneurs of Amsterdam and Zaandam. On their frequent visits to Amsterdam they were able to buy fine things made there as well as imported luxuries such as porcelain from China and

Japan and chintzes from India, to say nothing of picking up the latest fashions in furniture and interior decoration generally. Thus they shared the taste for richly carved oak furniture that developed during the seventeenth century amongst the wealthier inhabitants of Holland and Friesland (cf. the fine cupboard in this room) and also in the fashion for painted furniture which became popular in the towns around the Zuyder Zee towards the end of the century. The cupboard beds here show how people liked to have large wooden surfaces embellished with pictures copied from Bible illustrations or scenes of everyday life, the theme in this case being various aspects of rope-making, a trade of the utmost importance to seafarers. Few pieces of furniture escaped elaborate decoration at this time except, curiously enough, chairs which in Hindeloopen were generally

Folding table

painted in plain colours only.

If, however, the people of Hindeloopen were merely participating in the general taste of various periods, how was it that rooms like this, which one might have seen in any number of places in the past, came to be regarded as typical Hindeloopen interiors? The answer would seem to be that due to a marked decline in Amsterdam's trade around 1800, Hindeloopen shrank from a prosperous adjunct of the capital to an isolated fishing village which at the same time had little in common with the farming community throughout the rest of Friesland. As a result the style of its houses crystallized, so that when the first tourists appeared on the scene around 1880, it was almost inevitable that they should think of it as something unique to Hindeloopen. In the event this enabled the Hindeloopers to develop a considerable industry in painted furniture which was primarily produced for outsiders.

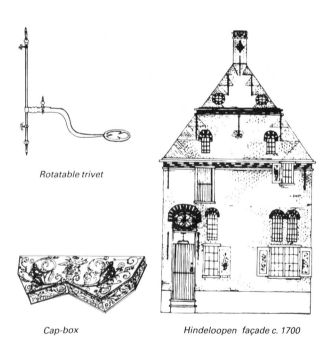

Rotatable trivet

Cap-box

Hindeloopen façade c. 1700

87 Horse mill for groats, Wormerveer (N.H.)

In the Low Countries groats, i.e. the hulled and coarse-ground grains of cereals, were mainly prepared from buckwheat. They were a very cheap and hence staple food, especially before the widespread acceptance of the potato. Mostly they were used for making gruel and porridge, and people still use them nowadays to make a semolina-type pudding. Up to the beginning of the nine-teenth century there were hundreds of groat mills in towns and villages throughout the country, each with its own shop run by the owner and one of his sons, or perhaps an assistant, doing a thriving local trade. The machinery in this mill dates from about 1770 and re-mained in use at Wormerveer until 1921. The building in which it is housed is not original.

Mill bill

As will be seen from the accompanying diagram, all the machinery was actuated by means of wooden pinions, belts and pulleys running off a large wooden cogwheel (T) pivoted on an upright wooden shaft (S), which was turned by one or, when operating to capacity, two horses (P).

First, however, the buckwheat, which the miller bought from the corn chandler, was roasted on a perforated iron tray (E) over a brick kiln (0). It was then transferred to a multiple sieve, or sifter (BZ), and from there fed to a

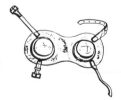

Blinkers

121

Runner

*Stone-dressing
reminder board*

groat crusher (A) containing a pair of furrowed stones, the upper one of which (the runner) was rotated so that the grains were crushed and roughly broken. The resulting grits, as they were termed, passed to another sifter, called a jumper (BRZ), where they were graded into different sizes (qualities), and finally the various grades were purified of any remaining husks and dusts in one of the three groat machines (W).

A groat machine consists of a simple casing with a fan inside to blow out lighter particles and is similar to the winnowing machines used on farms to separate the chaff from the grain after threshing. The farm machine, however, usually had to be worked by hand and by no means every farmer had one. Those without had to resort to the use of winnowing baskets with which they tossed the threshed grain in the wind so that the light chaff was carried away and only the heavy kernels were left behind. Besides groats, the mill also supplied buckwheat flour (for pancakes, etc.), cattle feed and mustard. The flour was done with another pair of stones (C) similar to the first but with different furrowing, so that the grain was ground rather than merely crushed. It was then dressed (separated from the meal in two bolters (BM) containing sieves of fine cloth stretched on rotatable reels. The grain for cattle feed was broken with a third pair of stones (B), while the mustard seed was pulverized with a fourth (D).

All the stones had to be dressed (sharpened) regularly, with the aid of a mill bill, and there is even a board to remind the miller when the next 'servicing' was needed.

Nameplate

Cross-section

Plan

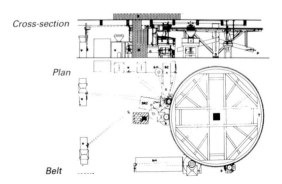

Belt

88   Farmhouse, Arnhem (Gld.)

As well as innumerable smallholdings there were of
course larger farmsteads on the Veluwe. This one is a
characteristic example of a type still to be seen in
considerable numbers between, say, Arnhem and
Zutphen. It is the only farmhouse in the museum not to
have been brought from elsewhere, having been built
on the spot around 1800. Although in form it is basically
the same as the farmhouse from Vierhouten (3), one can
clearly see, even from the outside, that more attention
has been paid to living conditions. The windows are
larger and there are more of them, and since there is
enough space for a passageway, the front door does not
have to open directly into the living-room.
The building is not open to visitors.

Fanlight

Wall clamp

89   Paper-mill from the Veluwe (Gld.)

This water-mill gives some idea of the type of mill that was still being used for papermaking in the mid-nine-teenth century in the old-established industrial area of the Veluwezoom, on the eastern edge of the Veluwe plateau. The overshot wheel (i.e. a wheel turned by water falling from above) drives a heavy wooden camshaft which works large wooden drophammers inside the building. Under these hammers linen rags are reduced to a pulp which is subsequently fed to the 'Hollander'. This is an oval tub where the pulp is cut up even more finely by a revolving cylinder set with steel blades. The fibres are then scooped out of the tub on a fine copper-wire screen and allowed to strain. After straining, the resulting sheet is carefully lifted off, placed in a press between felt pads to absorb the remaining moisture, and finally hung up to dry in the vented loft. A business the size of this mill will not have employed many people, but there were many places much larger.

The invention of printing at the end of the fifteenth century brought a considerable increase in the demand for paper, which up to then had been imported. Imported paper, however, was so expensive that people were soon trying to find ways of making it locally, and once again, as in the case of linen weaving (56), immigrants from the south played a major role. In fact they can be

124

said to have set Dutch papermaking on its feet, since the technology they brought with them was virtually unknown in the north. (In this they clearly differed from the immigrant textile workers who, when they came, joined an existing industry).

At first attempts were made to set up mills elsewhere in the country, probably in windmills, which at that stage were still not fully developed. But then, about 1600, attention turned to the Veluwe, which seemed to satisfy all the needs of this capital-intensive industry: pure water for the pulp, and also enough of it to power water-mills, which by that time had become well established in the region, so that there was an appreciable pool of experience to draw on. By 1650 there were as many as 28 paper mills in the area round Apeldoorn, and by 1740, when the industry was at its height, there were 174 of

Screen

them on the Veluwe as a whole, quite apart from numerous other types of industrial water-mills.

In the meantime, about 1670, producers had begun to show much greater interest in the better quality types of paper. This was particularly evident in the Zaan area to the north of Amsterdam, where windmills were used, and indeed by then the windmill had come into its own, being capable of virtually continuous production with the result that it had become the universal engine for industrial processes. In the nineteenth century, however, most of these mills missed out on the next wave of industrial development (steam, improvements in mass

125

production, etc.) and as a result all the paper-mills in the Zaan area disappeared. Some of those on the Veluwe managed to carry on as laundries, but the irony of it is that the paper they had produced had been partly responsible – as the bearer of printed information – for the rapid scientific progress that led to the downfall of their traditional methods.

Literature: C.Th. Kokke, De Veluwse papiermolen, 1977. With a summary in English (available in museum shop and kiosk)

90 Tower mill, Delft (Z.H.)

This mill, which is about 26 metres high, is in the form of a brick tower with a wooden stage round it and a thatched cap to carry the sails. The stage was used for setting the sail and also for winding. As with the post mill (55), winding was done by means of a winch on the end of the tail, but in this case the tail is a triangular set of braces reaching down to the stage and only the cap and sails were turned. The mill is thus a smock windmill. It was built around 1700 and until 1900 repeatedly altered and adapted. The inside consists of a number of floors with four sets of millstones (55). The equipment in the mill is rather similar to that in the horse mill described at 87.

The principle of the rotating cap was invented towards the end of the sixteenth century and from then on brick tower mills steadily ousted the cramped and limited post mills, especially in the west of the country. To catch sufficient wind, particularly in the towns, higher and higher towers had to be built, with the result that there was often not only room for the miller to live on the premises but more space to build extra floors for the accommodation of all kinds of wind-powered machinery. The development was also helped along by the growing sophistication in the use of gears, and as a consequence the tower mill came to be the type most commonly employed for industrial purposes in the towns. In fact tower mills used to be quite a feature of places like Rotterdam, Schiedam and Delft, many of them in the service of breweries.

The mosaic floor which is accomodated in the mill was originally part of the kitchen-cum-living room of the farm 'Erve Luttekes' in Hupsel nearby Winterswijk, which was destroyed by fire in 1937. Written in this floor are the date 1837 and the initials J R M G A L K: Jan RuMate and Grada Aleida LutteKes. In addition a heart, stars, and geometrical shapes can be distinguished (see also 11).

At the original site, c. 1910

127

91 War memorial

This memorial commemorates the evacuation of Arnhem in 1944 during the Second World War. It was made by Jerome Symons and presented to the museum at the commemoration in 1984 by ex-evacuees who had lived there from September 1944 to January 1945.

Arnhem had to be evacuated in 1944, because it had become part of the front line after the Allies' airborne landing to the north-west of the town (Operation Market Garden).

Most of the inhabitants made their way towards Apeldoorn, but many remained in the neighbourhood in hope of a speedy liberation. Hence around 600 people from the neighbouring residential areas decided to take shelter in the Open-Air Museum, occupying virtually all the buildings, down to the turf cabin and the fowler's hut.

But this refuge so close to the battlefield was not free from danger. Two days after their arrival one of the evacuees was killed by a piece of shrapnel, while in addition they had to look on helplessly while their houses in the town were looted by the Germans. On the morning of 3 October 1944 German soldiers burst in, killing Anton Zwiers, a resistance fighter, in the wood behind the tower mill from Delft. Most of the evacuees had to leave the museum terrain that day. Only a small number remained behind to experience the births of three children in the weeks that followed and to celebrate the feast of St. Nicholas and Christmas together in the museum.

At the end of December 1944 they too had to move on elsewhere. All in all their stay in the museum had lasted longer than anyone had originally imagined. The museum, severely damaged by the fall of a V1 and the digging of trenches, was liberated on 15 April 1945.

Reserve numbers 92-95

96 Dutch Reformed church, 's-Heerenhoek (Zld.)

Simple small church, built in 1672 and on a number of occasions since then partly restored. Originally it had a hipped roof; in 1832 the present, higher, facade was installed and the roof was extended behind it. At the same time the arched ceiling and likewise the two exterior windows in both side walls were installed. In 1888 the beams supporting the originally flat ceiling were sawn through and replaced with iron tie rods. In this way members of the congregation sitting in the balcony above the church door could also see the christening font. The pulpit is original; the christening rail and the pews are reconstructed based on the remainder of the design as it was at the beginning of this century. During services the men and women sat apart, the men in the pews along the side walls, and the women in the middle. In the winter the building was heated by footstoves which were placed between the pews before the service. In the second half of the last century a heater was installed with a pipe right across the ceiling. The vestry behind the church was built in 1929. From 1752 until 1915 a small school had stood there.

After the Reformation the originally Reformed, later known as Dutch Reformed religion was protected and supported by the Councils of Holland and Zeeland, through the exclusion of all other religions. The church administration consisted of stewards, who were appointed through the shires. For them, just as for the sheriffs and the aldermen (the local council), distinguished seats were reserved in church on either side of the pulpit.

After the Batavian Revolution in 1795 and the subsequent statutory equal rights given to the different religions, management and maintenance was passed on to the church councils themselves. Also through the area becoming Catholic, the Reformed congregation in 's-Heerenhoek was rather small and relatively poverty stricken. Therefore the church lacked an organ, only in 1902 was a harmonium acquired which was equipped with an imitation organ front. In the eighteenth century burials took place in church. This occurred in this church mostly in the ground under the flagstones, but there was also a special vault under the gravestones which can still be seen close to the pulpit.

At the original site, c. 1983

97   Farmstead, Etten en Leur (N.B.)

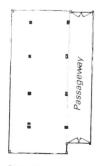

Plan of barn

Cross-section of barn

The main building dates from c. 1700, with later alterations. The living quarters are built entirely of brick but the aisled barn behind has wooden walls. The farming here was mixed, with some cattle and some arable land. In about 1750 the acreage was increased and a separate barn was built to cope with the increased arable yield. A bakehouse (116) was also added. House and shed are in use as exhibition areas.

The large freestanding barn is again in the form of a nave with two aisles (76). The nave in this instance, however, served as a 'mow', where grain and hay were stacked from the floor to the roof, and threshing (76) was done in one of the aisles, which also served as a through passageway for carts. This sort of barn, which could vary considerably in size, was known as a 'Flemish barn' since it was common in the Belgian part of De Kempen as well as in adjacent parts of North Brabant. In fact the areas on both sides of the border had a common culture, as is very obvious when one compares this Dutch farmhouse with the many examples, both large and small, in the Bokrijk Open-Air Museum near Hasselt in Belgium.

98 Farmhouse, Budel (N.B.)

This long, aisled building (76) comes from the Dutch part of De Kempen, an area straddling the border with Belgium, and some of the details of its construction suggest that it may go back to 1700. All the walls are brick. In the front wall are the door and window of the living room, and along one of the side walls is a series of doors giving on to, from right to left, the kitchen, the sunken stall (76) for cattle, the threshing-floor (76) and the sunken stall for sheep. Originally it was quite a large farm for the area, concentrating on arable crops such as cereals, to be sent to market, and large quantities of green fodder for the cattle and sheep, which supplied manure for the poor soil; however, there was a certain amount of dairy produce as well. Some time after 1800 it was reduced to a smallholding with only two or three cows, a draught ox and a few sheep, and the original arrangements of living quarters and barn was altered to a certain extent.

All the aisled barns (76) discussed so far have been arranged in more or less the same way: a threshing-floor in the centre, underneath a loft where hay or cereals were stored; stalls in the aisles; and the main entrance in the end wall, generally facing the road. After about 1700, however, another type of arrangement became quite common, not only in Brabant but also in other areas such as Drenthe and north-east Overijssel, on farms where the need for large quantities of manure was the most important consideration. Here the sunken stalls were dug in the nave and the side walls were made

Type of andiron

Hour glass

133

Chair

higher to take doors through which carts could be driven right into the stalls, either to empty them or bring a fresh layer of turves. At the same time this meant that windows and doors for the living quarters could also be let into the higher walls, as in this particular farm where the entrance to the kitchen is in the side wall towards the road.

To make the ceiling of this kitchen the spaces between the beams have been filled in with twigs bent round to form arches and plastered with clay. In the fireplace there is a wooden crane and hanger for the pot used to boil up fodder for the animals. The cupboard beds are decorated with a rustic form of Renaissance ornament and may date from the first phase of building around 1700.

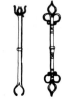

Wall clamps

Salt-box

Kitchen interior of the farm from Budel

Lantern

134

Barn doors at the back

Barn doors at the side

Kitchen interior of a seventeenth century farm in Nieuw-Ginneken (N.B.), 1966

Sunken stall of a seventeenth century farm in Nieuw-Ginneken (N.B.), 1966

Brood in schieten.

Bringing bread into the oven. Detail from a children's illustration
'Het Bakkersbedrijf', published by G. L. Funke, Amsterdam, c. 1870

99 Brewery and bakehouse, Ulvenhout (N.B.)

This building from Ulvenhout, together with its contents, most of which are from Sint-Oedenrode, gives some idea of a small village brewery as it might have looked in the nineteenth century. Like most country breweries in Brabant, it was attached to an inn ('De Roskam', now demolished), and usually the proprietor of such an establishment was one of the more prosperous inhabitants of the village, supplying beer not only for his own tavern but also for others nearby which did not have a brewery themselves but which may have had a small farm attached instead. There is a bakehouse built on at the side.

Paddle for stirring

Beer used to be the normal drink for most people, and Dutch beer, especially from the west of the country, was renowned both at home and abroad. The reputation of breweries like those in Haarlem, Gouda and Delft, for example, was already well established as far back as the fifteenth century, and the duty raised on the beer they sold was an important economic factor. Apart from the 'merchant' breweries, however, there were also the 'home' breweries, which produced beer for their own use and for others in the neighbourhood. Mostly run by women, they were to be found almost everywhere, in towns and villages as well as scattered about the countryside; so it is not surprising that they should have

Grain shovel

Beer barrel

Hop

fallen foul of the larger concerns from time to time, until eventually their activities were restricted by law. But then gradually, from about 1600 on, the restrictions were relaxed again, and in the eighteenth and nineteenth centuries every little town, village and hamlet in Brabant and Limburg had its own brewery, with its own special brew.

The process of brewing is based on a chemical reaction in which starch is converted into sugar and thence into alcohol. The material normally used to provide the starch was barley. This was first softened by being steeped in a bath of water (A) and then spread out on a floor (B) where it was kept moist and continually turned in order to promote germination and prevent the development of mildew. During germination some of the starch in the barley was converted into soluble sugar, but this was subsequently stopped by drying on a metal

rack in a oast-kiln (C). The dry, germinated grain (malt) was ground or crushed, dressed (i.e. purified), and then transferred to a tun (D) where it was mashed. This was done by adding hot water from a large copper heated over a brick oven (E) and stirring thoroughly so that the sugars dissolved. The resulting pulp (the mash) was drawn off into a tub (F) (leaving behind a sediment to be used as cattle feed) and from here it was pumped up into tanks in the loft, where vents in the roof ensured rapid cooling.

After cooling, the mash was run down into the copper (E), where it was boiled to give what was known as the wort, and perhaps hops would be mixed in to give it a bitter taste. The wort was then taken via the sump (F), pump and cooling tanks again, to the fermenting vat (I), where the sugars were fermented with yeast, to give alcohol and carbon dioxide. However, before the fermentation had actually stopped the liquor from the vat was drawn off into barrels and the process was allowed to continue while these were stored in the cellar (J) waiting to be delivered. Thus the finished beer was the result of hours of effort requiring both skill and judgement, and it was this of course which ultimately determined its flavour and quality.

Yoke for carrying barrels

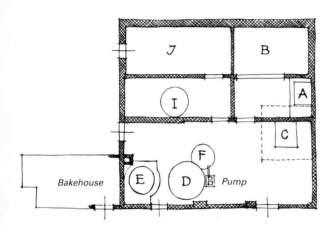

100　Farmstead, Krawinkel (L.)

Bench

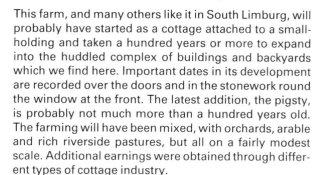

Lintel

This farm, and many others like it in South Limburg, will probably have started as a cottage attached to a small-holding and taken a hundred years or more to expand into the huddled complex of buildings and backyards which we find here. Important dates in its development are recorded over the doors and in the stonework round the window at the front. The latest addition, the pigsty, is probably not much more than a hundred years old. The farming will have been mixed, with orchards, arable and rich riverside pastures, but all on a fairly modest scale. Additional earnings were obtained through different types of cottage industry.

Most of the buildings here are based on a simple aisle-less framework (103), but many of the wattle-and-daub panels have been redone with **bricks**. As bricks became cheaper, or the farmer more prosperous, this seems to have been a fairly common practice when a farm needed renovating, especially on the higher ground in the east of the country and in South Limburg. In the present instance, even part of the timber frame has been replaced by brickwork.

Brick, of course, had always been much more respect-able than wattle and daub, and in the eighteenth and nineteenth centuries many an old wattle-and-daub building was given a brick façade, thereby altering the character of numerous village streets in South Limburg where the rows of brick-fronted farms became a very distinctive feature. Behind the smart façade, however, the old huddle of buildings, lean-tos and sheds remained unaltered. Thus, from the street, this farm would appear to be a broad, brick-built affair. But on passing through the gate on the right we find a long, rather narrow timber-framed house with a series of outhouses. In the farmhouse itself, the room at the front used to be the 'best room', reserved for special occasions. It has clayplastered walls and ceiling and is furnished in the style fashionable at the beginning of this century. From here a small doorway opens into the kitchen, with its open fireplace, which was where the family normally lived.

Leading off the kitchen is a small bedroom with a cupboard bed, and beyond this the back-kitchen and cellar where, among other things, the milk from the goats and the farm's small herd of cows was made into butter for

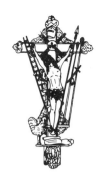

Crucifix

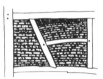

Brickwork panelling

sale in the neighbouring town. The usual earthenware vessels are stacked in the cupboard. There is also a bench of the type that was once quite common in simple dwellings but tended to persist in South Limburg longer than anywhere else. The brick fireplace was used to boil up fodder which was then taken out to the sheds on a small trolley.

The back-kitchen looks out across the main farmyard (with its dung heap) to the privy, pigsties, stables, byres and barns for storing hay and the harvest. On the other side of the house is another yard, for the cart; at the front

Wooden bench

141

Keystone

Trolley

there is a covered well, and at the back a bakehouse for baking bread and pastry.

A farm of this size will usually have provided the farmer and his family with little more than a bare subsistence, which they will have been compelled to eke out with money earned as labourers on the other farms and as seasonal workers in quarries across the border, or from weaving and making simple wrought ironwork for the German market.

101 Roadside shrine, Margraten (L.)

This shrine made of marl stood originally at a crossroads outside the village.
Many crucifixes and shrines were to be found in partic-
ular in Limburg, at prominent places such as three

forked roads and rising ground, but also alongside a road or in a field. They were dedicated to Mary or to a saint. The crucifixes and shrines were mainly erected by private individuals after a cure, prayers that had been answered or as a special dedication to a particular saint. A sudden death caused by an accident, a lightning strike, or a murder could be a reason for shrines being erected at a particular spot. There was a patron saint for each affliction or miraculous occurrence. The oldest shrines date from the fifteenth or sixteenth centuries.

102   Boundary post, Roosteren-Susteren (L.)

This post dating from possibly before 1600, stood on the boundary between the Duchies of Gelre and Gulik, which since 1839 have been part of the Dutch province of Limburg.

Plate, known as 'boeren Delfts', c. 1800

Church footstove painted in the Hindelooper style, dated 1890

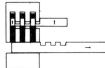

Bolt withdrawn

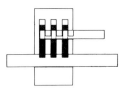

Bolt locked

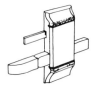

Wooden lock

103   Outhouse, Terstraeten (L.)

This outhouse, built about 1800, is a good example of a **timber-framed construction**, with walls filled in with **wattle and daub**. Inside are presses, tubs and pans for making syrup from apples and pears. This used to be a common rural industry in South Limburg, a traditional fruit-growing area.

Frame structures are still very much a feature of modern building. Nowadays steel and reinforced concrete are mostly used, but for centuries the load-bearing framework of houses, barns and sheds was made of wood, fashioned by the local carpenter, or wright. The framework of this particular building, clearly visible both the inside and the outside, gives a good idea of how it was done. First, a series of **transverse frames** were constructed, each consisting of two stout poles joined by a tie-beam anchored on the outside with wooden pegs. (In this building there are five such frames.) These were then hoisted, or 'reared', into an upright position, one behind the other, and made firm round the outer walls by means of crossbeams and braces, to form the familiar grid pattern in which door and window frames were completely integrated.

On the tie-beams, **roof-trusses** were mounted (though the end-trusses were sometimes omitted, as in this case). To make these, conveniently curved trunks or branches were sawn lengthwise with a long two-handed saw, so as to produce two symmetrical timbers like those used in shipbuilding. Once in position, the trusses were tied by a ridge pole and purlins, to which rafters were fastened with wooden pegs. The rafters were then covered with thatch, or laths and tiles, as required.

Such a construction, basically a **simple nave without aisles** was common in South Limburg.

The filling-in of the walls with wattle was carried out by twisting upright laths into grooves notched in the cross-timbers, and cross-weaving them with twigs or brushwood to form a close hurdling. The whole family, with their friends, would then probably lend a hand smearing the wattle with layers of daub, which consisted of a pulp of clay, chopped straw and cow-dung. Different recipes, of course, were used at different times and there were variations from district to district, but when finished, the cellular structures of such a wall, with its numerous pockets of air, would provide excellent insulation, well protected against the elements by the overhanging eaves.

The wooden locks on the two left-hand doors would seem to be prototypes of the modern Yale lock. In fact, locks like this used to be quite common all over the world, which only goes to prove there is virtually nothing new under the sun.

Transverse frame
1. tie-beam
2. posts

Grid
3. cross-beams
4. braces

Roof-truss
on tie-beam

Roof-truss 5. ridge pool
6. purlins
7. rafters

Wattle hurdling

Cross-section through
wattle and daub

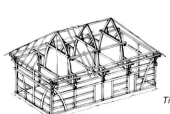

Timber framework outhouse

147

104   Archery butts,
Roermond (L.)

This archery range is a reconstruction of the archery butts 'De Roos', which was founded in 1889 in Roermond-Kapel. At each end of the double range there are targets. These consist of bales of straw, in front of which the actual target, the 'butt', hangs. The 'butt' is made of rolled up bundles of straw. The paper target area is fastened on the straw circle (diameter 75 cm) with four pins. On the range there are three rows of long and narrow planks, between which shooting was done. Any stray arrows ended up in these planks.
The distance between the place one shot from to the target was twenty-six metres. This was laid down.

Already in the prehistorical age bow and arrow had been used by man as a hunting and war weapon, as borne out by old cave drawings. Archery as a sport is probably a more recent phenomenon, but already even in the Middle Ages shooting associations existed in The Netherlands. Especially in the southern provinces target shooting was a widespread entertainment, at which hearty drinking mostly took place as well. Today the sport is still practised, all be it with rules that have changed with the passage of time. The principle of using the bow and arrow to shoot at a target, has however remained the same. Since 1972 archery has been an event at the Olympic Games.

Archer with longbow, 1933

105   Wagon hall

Pottery household equipment, c. 1650-1800

106 Auditorium

Slide-shows, exhibitions, and conference room. The basement of the auditorium contains the museum's earthenware collection in an open depot display. Earthenware objects were indispensable to housekeeping until well into the present century. Earthenware pots were used for cooking, for preserving fruit and vegetables and for storing things like foodstuffs and tobacco. Liquids were kept in earthenware jugs and bottles. Such utensils have largely been replaced over the course of time by objects in other materials, such as cast-iron, aluminium and various synthetics.

The earthenware collection comprises objects of very diverse types from different periods, ranging from medieval utensils to modern services. Earthenware can be seen in its original context in the furnished houses and workshops.

Reserve numbers 107-111

112 Summer-house, Meppel (Dr.)

From the beginning of the seventeenth century similar pavilions to this were built at the country seat of the well-to-do, especially in the province of Holland. They were part of stately gardens with avenues, hedges, arbours, fences, and walls, such as at the medieval residences of the nobility we come across in foreign countries.

The pavilions were originally situated against or as part of the garden fence, mostly in a corner or near the entrance gate. They served as a place outside the house from which one could enjoy a wide view of the landscape. Around the second half of the seventeenth century the location of these small buildings was no longer confined to the garden fence. They were now to be found for example at a point where two avenues crossed or at a striking location at the back of the garden. Frequently they were elevated a little by placing them

Ter plaatse, 1967   At the original site, c. 1967

on a mound or above a partially dug out cellar, or above a boathouse if they were situated alongside water. The extravagance of the decoration was dependant on the income of the owner, and comprised of plaster, ornaments, paintings of caves, statues, fountains, and the like. In the eighteenth century these pavilions materialised throughout the whole country. Sometimes, depending upon the fashion at the time, they took on a Chinese or Turkish form, but gradually they became more sombre in appearance. One drunk tea there, and on special occasions even something a little stronger. After 1800 new summer-houses were often covered with white plaster. This is also the case with the summer-house located on the small river Reest in Meppel, of which a partial replica has been set up in the museum. According to tradition the original was used for drinking teas and for parties. The original cellar with round windows and small steps leading to the door are not included in the museum's replica. The original building dates from 1860. Very few summer-houses like this one were built after this date. The Dutch name 'koepel' refers to its dome shape.

Koepel en hek van buitenplaats Roosendaal aan de vecht, 1917, detail van ets

Summer-house and fence at the country house of Roosendaal on the Vecht, 1719. Detail of an etching

113 Toll collector's house, Zuidlaren (Dr.)

This brick toll-house with a wooden toll-bar stood from
about 1850 on a paved road in Zuidlaren, close to the

Cabinet

boundary between Groningen and Drenthe (57).
The fairly large, dark red bricks used here are characteristic of the area, but the roof, with its decorative tiling, overhanging eaves and monumental chimney is rather distinctive and serves to emphasize the vaguely official nature of the building. The thousands of toll houses that used to bar the roads not only made many goods more expensive for the consumer but also caused considerable delays, which was why the keeper often ran an inn or tavern as well. The right to levy tolls was usually granted by licence.

Toll-bar with toll-house, Bedum, c. 1935

Coffee urn

Frisian long-case clock

TOLTARIEF

op den **STEENWEG** tusschen den grooten weg der eerste klasse No. 1 bezuiden de gemeente **HAREN** en de gemeente **ZUIDLAREN.**

Bij de aankomst aan een der tolboomen zal voor tol moeten worden betaald:

Voor rij- of voertuigen met *vier* wielen voor elk aangespannen paard, ezel, muilezel of runderbeest	f 0.15
Voor rij- of voertuigen met *twee* wielen, mitsgaders sleden, voor elk aangespannen paard, ezel, muilezel of runderbeest	- 0.10
Drie wielen aan een rijtuig worden gerekend voor *vier.*	
Voor elk gezadeld paard of muilezel	- 0.07½
Voor elk paard, gespannen voor eene hessenkar met *twee* of *vierwielen*	- 0.30
Voor diligences of postwagens, ingerigt voor niet meer dan *zes* personen, voor elk paard	- 0.15
Voor meer dan *zes*, doch niet meer dan *negen* personen	- 0.17½
Idem, voor meer dan *negen* personen	- 0.20
Voor elken bok, geit of hond, gespannen voor rij- of voertuig met *twee* wielen	- 0.01½
Idem voor een rij- of voertuig met *vier* wielen	- 0.03

Voor de tolbetaling wegens bovengemelde voorwerpen zal een bewijs worden verstrekt, tegen afgifte waarvan men aan den *tweeden* tolboom van de betaling zal zijn vrijgesteld.
Wegens na te melden voorwerpen zal de tol aan ieder tolhek worden geheven zonder afgifte van bewijs en zal worden betaald:

Wegens elk los paard of muilezel	- 0.03
" " runderbeest of ezel	- 0.01½
" " schaap, kalf of varken	- 0.01
Wanneer een kudde schapen of varkens sterker is dan *vijftig* stuks in eens	- 0.50
Wegens bespannen boerenwagens, onverschillig waarmede geladen of geheel ongeladen, en hetzij naar Groningen gaande of vandaar terugkomende op de gewone weekmarktdagen der stad Groningen	- 0.02½
Wegens bespannen boerenwagens in de gevallen als boven op den nademiddag en avond voor die weekmarktdagen naar Groningen gaande	- 0.05

Hiervan zijn echter uitdrukkelijk uitgezonderd zoodanige boerenwagens of korrewagens, waarvan, uithoofde hunne zakanken op veren, nemen of andere rekbare lijchamen zijn geplaatst, de personele belasting op de paarden in hoogere klassen dan van landbouwers in verschuldigd of zoodanige boerenwagens, welke door gepatenteerde voerlieden gebruikt worden tot vervoer tegen vrachtloon van personen of goederen, welke alle aan het algemeen tarief van tol blijven onderworpen.
De bovenstaande bepalingen betrekkelijk den marktol zijn van geene toepassing op den Zuidlaarder heritemarktdag, wanneer die gelijk tot duurdere invalt op den Groninger weekmarktdag, en zal op dien dag de tol naar het gewoon tarief zonder onderscheid worden geheven. Dergelijks zullen tusschen beide de gabellen wonende particulieren evenzeer als ingezetenen van het gehucht GLIMMEN niet meer dan den halven tol verschuldigd zijn.
Indien een gedeelte van den Nederlandschen cent zal verschuldigd zijn, zal steeds een halve cent worden gevorderd.
Wanneer bij het ontstaan van doox weder na ingevallen vorst de passage op den grooten Rijksweg bij verordening van het Provinciaal of andere Besturen voor vrachtwagens mogt zijn gestremd, zullen zoodanige vrachtwagens gedurenden zoodanigen tijd op den onderwerpelijken weg NIET worden toegelaten, dan tegen betaling van den VIERDUBBELEN tol.

154

114 Boundary post of hunting ground, Arnhem (Gld.)

Boundaries of this kind delineated the limits of the area within which individuals had the right to hunt. On the west side of what currently is South Arnhem there used to stand two such posts, which indicated the hunting ground attached to the former manor of Meijnerswijk. One post stood close to the Rhine next to the southern land-abutment of what used to be a floating-bridge, the other stood at the Rijnbandijk between Elden and Driel. It was this latter post which was transferred to the Open-Air Museum in 1939. The inscription is as follows: 'Heerlijkheid Meijnerswijk Jachtpaal' (Boundary post of the hunting ground of the manor of Meijnerswijk).

The location of the post before being transferred to the museum was described as follows: 'Between hecto-metre posts numbers 175 and 176 at a distance of 22 metres and 40 centimetres from post number 175, which is to be found a little to the west of the exit from 'Elden-hof' farm.

Gable finials

115   Small farmhouse, Beuningen (Ov.)

This little los hoes (76), which comes from the eastern part of the province of Overijssel known as Twente, was built about 1700. It has half-timbered walls filled with wattle and daub (103) and oakplanked gables patterned with straw thatch. Details of how a farmhouse of this type was run are given at 76.

As in Drenthe the older farms in Twente are settled on the sandy soils found on the higher ground. Instead of being grouped together in villages, however, the farmhouses here were often scattered about the countryside, separated from their neighbours by woods and wasteland. They were usually quite large structures of the los hoes type and would have various smaller buildings nearby: a sheepcote, a bakehouse for breadmaking (116), perhaps a small water-mill and very often, at a later period, a cartshed. There might also have been a smaller los hoes, like this one, meant for elderly parents or for a farm labourer who was allowed to cultivate a small patch of land on his own account.

The economy of such a tiny farm was modest indeed. Each year a small plot was given over to the rye from which people made their own bread; a goat was kept for milk, a pig and a couple of sheep for meat and wool, and in the sunken stall in the aisle (76), one or two cows for their dung. Generally some flax was grown as well and this, like the wool from the sheep, was spun at home on a spinning-wheel. The thread was often woven at home too, but sometimes the village weaver was entrusted with this task. Virtually everything produced was for the household's own use, there being no significant surpluses of any kind, and no question of using horses or building up reserves.

Fireguard

As long as the small farm formed part of a larger production unit its inhabitants were ensured of a certain amount of protection against penury, crop failures and suchlike. When the population of Twente and the Achterhoek began to expand, however, many people started up independent farms of their own on small patches of unused and generally poor land, and due to the precarious nature of their existence soon lost virtually all they had, thereby giving rise to an early form of rural proletariat with nothing but its labour to offer in the struggle for survival. By 1700 or thereabouts this had already led to

Pot-hanger

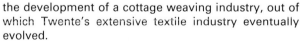

the development of a cottage weaving industry, out of which Twente's extensive textile industry eventually evolved.

The fireplace here is simply a pit in the floor of the house place, which is made of pebbles. The rotatable pot-hanger suspended over it could be used to support either a kettle for household use or a cauldron for boiling up cattle fodder. Cooking-pots would be placed on a trivet (Fig. 127) or simply stood on their own three legs among the glowing ashes. At night-time the fire was sometimes the only source of light, though it might be supplemented by a small oil- or fat-lamp. When people went to bed, it was damped down with turves and

Blowpipe

Cooking-pot

covered with a wrought-iron guard, and in the morning it was blown up again with an iron blowpipe or a pair of bellows. In the absence of a chimney the smoke had to find its own way out through cracks and crannies. The inhabitants slept on straw in the rough wooden cupboard beds in the aisles. They had to get their water from the well outside, using a counterbalanced beam to raise the bucket.

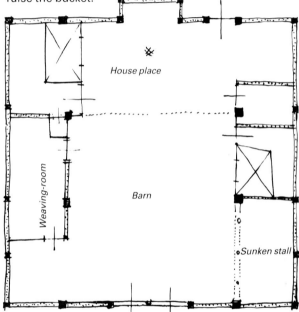

House place

Weaving-room

Barn

Sunken stall

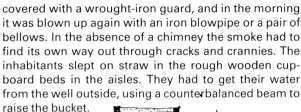

Kettle

Spinning-wheel

Well

Hand churn

116   Bakehouse, Denekamp (Ov.)

This bakehouse once stood near a large Twente los hoes. The date 1741 is carved over the door. Bakehouses were often built separately from the farmhouse because of the risk of fire. Most of the other examples in the museum simply consist of the bread-oven with a little roof over it, but this one is quite a large affair in which the oven occupies only a small part.

The **oven** is essentially a small chamber made of bricks and clay. This would be heated by lighting a fire of faggots inside, the mouth being left open to let the smoke out. When the bricks were hot enough, the fire would be raked out and the risen dough pushed inside with the aid of a peel. The oven would then be closed and the dough would bake in the heat retained by the bricks. Under the shelter by the side of this bakehouse bees were kept.

Lintel

Dough trough

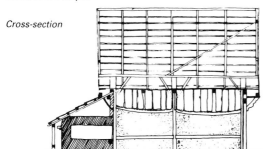

Cross-section

Peel

117 Small drainage mill, Wouterswoude (Fr.)

This type of mill, known locally a **tjasker**, is a wind-driven adaptation of an Archimedes' screw. It is designed to pump water up out of low-lying waterlogged meadowland into a wooden drainage gully which flows out on the other side of the dike. This example was built about 1870.

The screw is encased in a hollow open-ended cylinder and is erected in a slanting position so that its foot is immersed in a small bowl-shaped reservoir into which, in the normal way, water from a whole grid of drainage channels would flow. The screw is directly driven by the sails mounted on the end of the shaft. When rotated, it raises the water up through the casing and spills it into the wooden gully. To stop the mill turning, there is a brake just behind the sails. This is a band brake, in which the band (gripe) acts on the rim of the brakewheel mounted on the shaft. A device like this is found in all mills but is not usually visible as it is mounted on the windshaft up in the cap. So that the mill can be pushed round into the wind, the frame (buck) which supports the shaft runs on rollers over a wooden rail. In actual practice both the rail and the wooden gully form a complete circle but only a section has been set up in the museum.

A small windmill of this type would only take about three weeks to build, and even simpler versions, worked by hand, were made too. Large numbers continued to be built right up until about 1930, most of them being made for farmers in Friesland. West Groningen, Drenthe and the northern part of Overijssel, who used them to drain their lowest meadows (usually 3 to 4 hectares, i.e. about 8 to 10 acres). In winter this land was normally left flooded and the mills were often wholly or partly dismantled and stacked away until the spring. Apart from farmers, however, peatmen also found a use for them in keeping down the level of ground water in the deep pits dug in the peat banks.

118   Small drainage mill, Gorredijk (Fr.)

All the machinery in this mill, which was built in the nineteenth century, is wooden. Like the tjasker (117), it has a screw mounted in a slanting position, with its foot in the water. The casing here, however, is on the ground and open at the top. The water which is pumped up flows over a low weir into a spillway on the other side of the dike.

This type of mill is known as a hollow post mill. Both in construction and in the method of winding the sails into the wind, it is very similar to the conventional post mill (55), but as its name suggests the post on which it rotates is not solid but hollow. Through this runs a wooden shaft which transmits the driving force of the wind on the sails to the gears connected to the screw.
These mills were mainly found in Friesland and like the tjasker were mostly owned by farmers. They were more expensive and were not very powerful, but the running gear was more protected from the elements. Even so, they still had to be wound by hand and people sometimes had to come quite a long way to do it.

Reserve numbers 119-124

Hollow post-mill near Raard (Fr.), 1900. Pencil drawing by Ids Wiersma, Friesland Museum collection, Leeuwarden

Archimedian screw of a hollow post-mill

125 Costume hall

The Open-Air Museum accomodates two large collections of clothes and jewellery. One of these collections is the museum's own property, the other is the property of the Foundation of Historical Collections of the House of Orange-Nassau.

In the past the collection of clothes and jewellery was mainly on the basis of regional differences and the magnificence and splendour of the costumes. The emphasis lay then on regional costumes which led to the Open-Air Museum boasting the largest collection of regional costumes in The Netherlands. These days, not only with the acquisition but also in the presentation the emphasis is placed on the similarities and differences in style and material between regional costumes and current fashion, on the social and economic background, and on the manner of manufacture and design. For this reason it is no longer only regional costumes and jewellery, and then mainly Sunday clothes, which are collected, but also working clothes and fashionable clothes in relation to regional costumes.

Since 1949 the Open-Air Museum has on loan the collection of regional costumes and jewellery belonging to the Foundation of Historical Collections of the House of Orange-Nassau. The present collection stems from an acquisition of regional costumes, which was given to Her Majesty Queen Wilhelmina on the occasion of her Golden Jubilee. The collection is still constantly being added to. This is the responsibility of the 'Queen Wilhelmina' Foundation of Dutch Regional Costumes.

In the in 1987 completely renovated and newly refurbished costume hall at the museum, there are varying exhibitions to visit, which are assembled from both collections.

126   Wood shed, Haarlem (N.H.)

Shed used for the storage of wood. In such wood sheds,
with both sides open to the wind, the timber lay sometimes for years to season. This shed was built around
1850 at a sawmill adjoining a timber and ship building
firm in Haarlem. It can only be viewed from the outside,
as it is used to store building materials for the museum.

127 Small farmhouse, Harreveld (Gld.)

The earliest record we have of this farm, which again is an aisled los hoes (76), dates from 1771 and the oldest parts of the building could also date from that period. When it was transferred to the museum, however, both exterior and interior were kept as they were found, in the form they had assumed in the course of the nineteenth century. Only the front wall is still done in wattle and daub, all the other outside walls being brick. The blue wash over the daub and on the clay walls inside was customary in this area, perhaps as a means of warding off flies.

Walking-frame

The scale and organization of the work on this little farm would have been much the same as described at 115, except that the stall for the cows is slightly larger (capable of taking three or five animals) and there is also a pigsty. To accomodate these the building has been extended at the back, past the last posts of the timber frame (103). During the course of the nineteenth century, animal husbandry came to take pride of place in the agriculture of the sandy soils in the eastern part of the country, with the result that arable farming was reduced to little more than the minimum necessary to feed the stock. By 1870 local markets had virtually ceased to handle field crops and were mainly devoted to such animal products as were in excess of the farmers' own needs.

Trivet

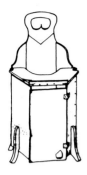

Baby's chair

Oil-lamp

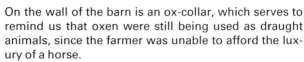

On the wall of the barn is an ox-collar, which serves to remind us that oxen were still being used as draught animals, since the farmer was unable to afford the luxury of a horse.

In the house place there is a forked tree-trunk attached to the ceiling. On this hang various implements for use in cooking and tending the fire, including an iron pot crane on which kettles or cauldrons could be suspended at various heights. Indications of a somewhat higher standard of living than that obtaining in the Twente los hoes (115) are the provision of more built-in cupboards, the better carpentry in the cupboard beds, and the presence of an inside privy and even two separate little rooms partitioned off in the aisles.

Even so, the inhabitants still could not hope to live solely on what the farm produced and were forced by dire necessity to engage in secondary activities, producing things not for themselves or the village community but

Flax brake

for trade further afield where better markets were to be found. Many of them even went away for a long period each year to work as wage-earners for large concerns elsewhere in the country or abroad. The importance of cottage industries is plainly to be seen in this farmstead, both from the large area devoted to a weaving-room, capable of accommodating two looms, and from the presence on the premises of a wheelwright's shop (128). Other local industries apart from weaving and the making of cartwheels included the making of clogs, shoes and brushes, woodturning, and digging for iron ore. In the woods oak-bark was collected for the local tanneries, and there was also a certain amount of charcoal burning to provide fuel for the iron foundries and other industries in the region.

Pot crane

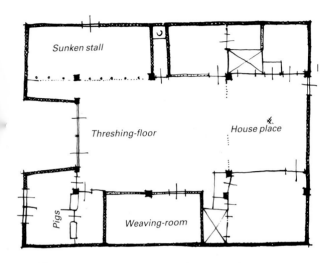

Waffle iron

Ox-collar

The weaver Lute Slotboom at work, c. 1917 pen drawing by Ids Wiersma

Jug cutter

At the original site, c. 1900

128 Wheelwright's shop, 't Woold (Gld.)

As a craft, wheelmaking was one of the most developed forms of cottage industry. In this workshop wheels were made for carts and wagons, sometimes to the order of a farmer in the neighbourhood, but more often for dealers in such places as Deventer, who had a wide market for

all sorts of farming gear, including things like winnowing baskets, wooden shoes, seed skeps, flails (76),
sieves, brushes, tubs and barrels. There were numerous
wheelwrights' shops in the Achterhoek, particularly
around Winterswijk; records of them go back to before
1800 and in 1870 there were still several dozen in operation. They were often attached to farms, which helped
to provide the basic necessities of life but were usually
of secondary importance (127).

The Achterhoek was a richly wooded area, with an
abundance of oaks and elms, and this was doubtless
one of the reasons why wheelmaking and other forms of
woodworking were so highly developed there.
Though easy to describe in a few words, the process of
making a wheel was one of the most difficult branches
of carpentry. The hub and spokes were made from oak
logs which were split and roughly hewn into shape on
the large chopping-block outside. The hub was then
finished off on a hand-operated lathe inside. The rim
(felloe) was made up of curved segments which were
cut from thick planks with a buck saw. The parts were
then carefully assembled and passed on to the smith
who provided an iron tyre for the rim and rings to streng-
then the hub. The finished wheels were carried to the
dealers by horse and cart or, later on, by train.

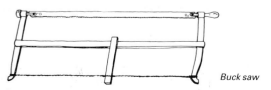

Buck saw

Historical landscape features on the museum terrain

Original landscape features

The museum's land has its own history and various traces of this are still to be found here. Before the museum was established on the site (in 1914), it was an estate called 'De Waterberg'. Avenues, woods and woodland pools still remind us of that.

The area has been under cultivation for three centuries, during which it was used for arable farming, animal husbandry and forestry. The large meadow in front of the restaurant was brought under cultivation from heathland in the 17th century. In the 18th century beech and pine woods were planted and the woodland pools and channel were dug out. The site is on the ice-pushed ridge or glacial moraine of the Southern Veluwezoom. This ridge was created in the Ice Age out of the soil the ice pushed in front of it. On the museum site it reached a height of about 80 metres N.A.P. (= Normal Amsterdam Level).

The beech and pine woods that now form part of the vegetation on the museum terrain were planted in the 19th century. On the highest part of the ridge to the south of the large meadow (between 113 and 116) there is a beechwood which is typical of the cultivated landscape of the southern edge of the Veluwe. The beeches here were all planted for timber production or for park planting. Such woods are becoming more and more rare, since many of them have been felled and replanted with other kinds of trees. In the museum this woodland area is maintained in being, so that an original and characteristic piece of the Gelderland landscape is

represented on the site.

There are few museum objects on this part of the site and visitors can enjoy a peaceful walk there. The high path offers a splendid view of the 'Zaan district' at several points (between 113 and 114).

In this wood there is a channel or spreng in the form of a long pool with a spring, another typical feature of the Veluwe push-moraine landscape. The spreng is a man-made watercourse which is fed by the ground water of the plateau, which naturally tends to run away at the sides. From the Middle Ages onwards such channels were dug out to drive watermills, for irrigating fields and probably also for the provision of drinking water.

The channels usually have banks of excavated soil on either side and are often sheet-piled. They were regularly maintained by the owners of watermills, which needed a constant supply of clear running water for such purposes as laundering and paper making. Thanks to the presence of channels and brooks, there grew up a prosperous paper industry in the area. A working example of a paper mill with a waterwheel is to be seen beside the woodland pool (89).

In the eighteenth and nineteenth centuries channels and brooks were often diverted to provide water for lakes and fountains in estates and parks. The channel on the museum site was dug out in the eighteenth century to beautify the estate and perhaps also to supply water. The brook that flowed from it through the large meadow has disappeared in the course of time. In 1984 the channel was deepend and sheet-piled again and the brook dug out across the meadow. The intention is to have its banks grazed by sheep, so that a wild vegetation will come into being as a contrast to that of the meadow beside it, which is cultivated with the aid of artificial fertilizer.

Added historical features

In the museum are to be seen buildings like houses, windmills and farmsteads, which once stood somewhere else in The Netherlands and have been transported to this terrain. In a number of instances features from various cultivated landscapes have been laid out as settings for these buildings. For example, around farmhouses there are farmyards, vegetable gardens, orchards, meadows and fields. With dykes, ponds, planting and ditches a suggestion is evoked of the landscapes in which the buildings in the museum really belong. Before the farmhouses from Friesland and Groningen were brought here, a flat landscape was created in what used to be an area of shifting sand with small dunes and pine trees.

In addition to these settings, historical landscape features have also been reconstructed. Around the Texel sheepcote (44) a **tuunwal** has been laid out, an enclosing bank of piled up turves. Banks of this type were common in the Frisian Islands and the Zuyder Zee area. They served to protect the meadows and keep the animals in, like the earthen banks customary elsewhere with their thick hedges of trees and bushes. Trees and bushes are hard to grow in the areas mentioned on account of the sea winds, hence this special kind of bank. Nowadays the tuunwal is found mainly on Texel, where it forms part of a protected cultivated landscape.

In the Drenthe section (75, 76, 77) there is a 'fire pond'. Round ponds of this kind in the middle of a village used to be a familar sight in the east of The Netherlands and in North Brabant. They were dug out as watering places for the animals on their ways to their stalls and they also served for washing the animals. Since there were many more of these ponds than were necessary for these purposes, it appears that they performed another important function, that of providing water for firefighting, no superfluous luxury in the past in view of the fire hazard presented by the numerous thatched roofs.

Old Dutch breeds of domestic animals

The animals on the terrain supplement the landscape features. Animals like chickens, sheep, pigs and horses are to be seen in a setting or near the buildings of the region to which they belong. They are all representatives of old Dutch breeds.

Domestic animals have long played an important role in the life of mankind. Their flesh was a direct source of food, while such products as milk and eggs were an addition to the daily diet and the yield of a piece of ground could also be improved with their manure. These animals further supplied man with products such as wool, feathers, horn, bone and leather for making utensils and clothing, while the horse was mainly used as a working and pack animal and for drawing carts.

Through the breeding of animals with different characteristics, various local breeds came into being which were adapted to life in given regions. There are sheep with thick fleeces for wool production, and on the other hand sheep mainly bred for meat production. In the heathlands on the poor sandy soils, however, sheep were as important for their manure as for meat or wool, and a type was bred there which offered all these things and which could yet live off the meagre grazing afforded by a heath. There are chickens which lay eggs nearly all year round and others which are not such good layers, but which provide plenty of good meat, an important source of income around big cities.

It is on account of these various characteristics that the animals constitute an important addition to the picture of the economic history of a region. As a result of changes in arable farming and animal husbandry some of these breeds have disappeared or become rare. The maintenance of surviving breeds in being also ensures the preservation of characteristics which might come to be of economic importance again in the future.

'Gaymanseik' at the spring, 1987

Information

Nederlands Openluchtmuseum
Schelmseweg 89
6816 SJ Arnhem
Telefoon (085) 57 61 11

Where and When?

The Netherlands Open-Air Museum lies close to the A12/E35 (Oberhausen-Utrecht) road on the northern edge of Arnhem.
It is easy to reach from Arnhem railway station by bus No. 13 (to Burger's Zoo).
The museum is open from 1 April to 1 November, from Monday to Friday from 9 a.m. – 5 p.m., and on Saturday and Sunday from 10 a.m. to 5 p.m.

Day trip No. 36 on Dutch Rail
(subject to alteration)

Information

For any queries, requests and complaints you can contact the information department. This department is located at the entrance to the museum (telephone number (085) 576333). Here you can inquire about the facilities for groups and guided tours, while at the same time you can also be brought into contact with the museum's curators.

Restaurant

The museum restaurant 'De Oude Bijenkorf' serves meals and drinks and caters for dinners, parties, receptions et cetera, even outside the normal opening times of the museum.
You can go to the Inn 'De Hanekamp' for a pancake.
Information concerning prices and reservations from: 'De Oude Bijenkorf' Schelmseweg 89, 6816 SJ Arnhem, (085) 42 06 57.

Further information:

- Information for parties and about other departments in the museum is available from the Information department.
- The museum restaurant 'De Oude Bijenkorf' serves meals and drinks. The 'Hanekamp' inn is the right place for a pancake.
  For information about prices and reservations, apply to: 'De Oude Bijenkorf', Schelmseweg 89,
  6816 SJ Arnhem, telephone (085) 57 64 57

- The museum cannot accept any liability for damage to people or property on the museum premises.
- Lost property should be reported to the head of museum services at the entrance.
- First aid: consult the staff at the entrance or warn the nearest museum attendant.
- Dogs must be kept on a lead.
- Amateurs may take photographs on the understanding that if they are published, the source will be acknowledged. Photographs for commercial purposes can only be taken with the permission of the management of the museum.

  Suggestions or complaints should be addressed to the head of museum services or to the Information department at the entrance.

The Society of Friends of the Open Air Museum assists the museum through financial support in achieving its objective. You can participate in this by becoming a member of the society. It entitles you to free entry to the museum and receipt of the magazine 'Bijdragen en Mededelingen' (with summaries in English), which is published twice a year.

The buildings listed below were given by or acquired with the financial assistance of the individuals or bodies mentioned.

- Fowler's hut (No. 2), R. de Favauge, Aerdenhout
- Small Veluwe farmhouse (No. 3), Mrs. M.C. ter Horst-Vogel, Schiedam
- Exhibition of bee-keeping (No. 4), Society of Friends of the Netherlands Open-Air Museum, Arnhem
- Sheepcote (No. 13) and dovecote (No. 21) evacués from Arnhem (1940-1945)
- Farmhouse from the Vollenhove district (No. 20), Baron Sloet tot Oldruitenborgh
- Double drawbridge (No. 33), Province of North-Holland
- Merchant's house (No. 34), N.V. Stijfselfabriek 'De Bijenkorf', formerly M.K. Honig, Koog on the Zaan
- Fisherman's cottage (No. 43) W. Dijserinck, Aerdenhout
- Eelmonger's hut (No. 46), City of Amsterdam
- Weighbridge and weighhouse (No. 66), C.J. van Damme, Kortgene
- Parish pump (No. 72) and farmhouse-inn 'De Hanekamp' (No. 74), City of Zwolle
- T.B. patient's hut (No. 81), Nationale Kruisvereniging, Bunnik
- War memorial 1944 (No. 91), ex-evacuees from Arnhem
- Paper mill (No. 89), Society of Dutch Paper Manufacturers
- Tower mill (No. 90), Frans-Holl. Oliefabrieken 'Calvé-Delft' and Nederlandse Gist- en Spiritusfabriek, Delft
- Dutch Reformed Church (No. 96), Municipality of Borsele
- Brewery and bakehouse (No. 99), Heineken's Bierbrouwerij-Maatschappij N.V. and Centraal Brouwerijkantoor, Amsterdam
- South Limburg farmstead (No. 100), National Coal-Mines

- Boundary stone (No. 102), Roosteren District Council
- Twente bakehouse (No. 116), A.J.H. Blijdestein, Enschede
- Small drainage mill (tjasker) (No. 117), H.P. Smids, Hardegarijp
- Small drainage mill (hollow post mill) (No. 118), E.J. Posthuma, Gorredijk
- Small Achterhoek farmhouse (No. 127), inhabitants of Lichtenvoorde and district

Interested in more open-air museums?
- Enkhuizen (N.H.), Rijksmuseum 'Zuiderzeemuseum'
- Barger Compascuum (Dr.), Veenmuseumdorp 't Aole Compas
- Bokrijk/Genk (Belg. Limburg), Vlaams Openluchtmuseum Bokrijk

There are Open-Air Museums in a great many other countries.

Related to the Netherlands Open-Air Museum are:
- Stoomhoutzagerij Nahuis, Groenlo (Gld),
- Boerenwagenmuseum, Buren (Gld.),
- Huize 'Keizer', Denekamp (Ov.).

Colophon

Text
J.M. Bos, E.M.Ch.F. Klijn et al.

Editors
Publication Committee Netherlands Open-Air Museum

Drawings
A.J. Aanstoot, W. Piek

Photographs
G.J. Derksen, J.M. Maassen, W.G.A. de Rooij,
J.M. Stikvoort, M.P. Wijdemans

Design
W.G.A. de Rooij

Published by
Uitgeverij Special Images b.v., Enschede

Translated by
Patricia Wardle, Alan Griffith, Nigel Browne